THE SPIRIT *of the*
GLACIER SPEAKS

ARKAN LUSHWALA

THE
SPIRIT
of the
GLACIER
SPEAKS

❖

ANCESTRAL TEACHINGS
OF THE ANDEAN WORLD FOR THE
TIME OF NATURAL DISORDER

DISRUPTION
BOOKS

Austin New York

Published by Disruption Books
New York, New York
www.disruptionbooks.com

Distributed by Disruption Books

For information about special discounts for bulk purchases, please contact Disruption Books at info@disruptionbooks.com.

Cover and book design by Brian Phillips Design

Library of Congress Cataloging-in-Publication Data available

Printed in the United States of America

Print ISBN: 978-1-63331-085-8
Ebook ISBN: 978-1-63331-086-5

First Edition

To my dear daughters,
Iohanna, Copalli, Maia, and Agatha

Contents

❖

THIRD DOOR: A GOOD WAY OF USING POWER

FOURTH DOOR: THE GIFT OF TIME

INTRODUCTION

❖

While singing to the spirits of the mountains and preparing sacred offerings to feed our Mother Earth, I am seeing the paths that the Universe has opened for us lately—paths of spiritual and human development that we are going to need to walk in order to continue living. In the midst of so many disasters affecting humanity, I have seen something beautiful that I can no longer hide. Even more, I feel a longing to give birth to something new. And as mothers know well, this can only be done with full conviction, like a whale that crosses an ocean. Among my convictions, one comes from my relationship with the ancestral world I grew up surrounded by, having been born in the Andes. I am convinced that anything new, to have real power, needs an ancestral root.

When seeking new and better solutions for the great social problems and natural catastrophes of the present moment, I believe that ancestral wisdom has more to offer than technological advances. Because technology does not have the ability to illuminate nor improve what lives inside people—the true source of the problems that are harming the world. Social injustice, the destruction of nature, excessive wealth, and extreme poverty come as a result of excessive human ambition. Such greed will not disappear with new technologies. We need greed to stop being fashionable, to cease being the marker of human progress. Only with wisdom will it be possible to resolve the problems of our time, with sensible cultural proposals that can help us aspire to reach happiness in another way. Therefore, I have no doubt that the ancestral wisdom of our Andean-Amazonian communities has much to contribute to the development of a new world culture.

Five hundred years ago, our ancestral culture could have become a part of the way of thinking that guides humankind. But in that moment, those who invaded our lands considered us pagans. Their religious beliefs did not permit them to see the precious contents of our sacred world. The Europeans of that time were not able to accept that there was wisdom in our culture. They were not even capable of learning from our ancestors, whom they considered inferior. But what if the sea brought them here because they needed to learn something? When I heard that an ocean current helped the Genovese merchant Christopher Columbus come to our shores, thinking he had arrived at another part of the world, the thought occurred to me that this was no accident. Our European brothers came here to be fed by something that our ancestral culture had to offer them, something that they needed after centuries of going from one war to the next.

Nature always does such things, connecting different parts of itself so that they may help one another. Europeans and the inhabitants of the ancient Andean-Amazonian world, as parts of nature and of the Earth, could have helped each other have more wisdom and a better way of life. Supposedly, the Europeans arrived in this part of the world in search of spices, and we had vast experience in the use of spices; we used spices as medicine, to improve the taste of life, and to remove bitterness from the heart. But sadly, shortly after arriving on our continent, the Europeans became aware that, in addition to spices, there were also precious metals here, and that got them distracted. Just as they lost interest in being healed by our food, they could no longer see our hearts. Their eyes sought only gold, and they could not see us. They saw our sacred world from afar and, afraid of it, did not come closer. Their lack of experience in the art of entering into good relationships did not allow them to love us. Their only experience was with fighting, and they waged a terrible war in order to legalize the theft of our lands through their triumph. And despite the fact that they made our lands their own, they were never able to know their true treasures. Given that those who cannot be satisfied also don't know how to stop, they didn't consider taking the time to get to know the deepest secrets and the real treasures of the place they had come to. They continued on their way, looking for something new to appropriate. If they had simply let themselves sit down for a moment amid the pastures of these lands, they might have felt something in their hearts, and they might have become enamored of the beautiful people here who were one with the land. But they were too busy and could not take notice of what lay right in front of them. And so they lost the chance of encountering our mother, the mother we all have in common, the one they had forgotten—our Mother Earth.

Coming from a world dominated by fearsome male authorities, how good it would have been for our European brothers to have felt the warmth of our mother, contained in the soups that we fed them when they arrived from their long journey, tired and shivering with cold. But they did not know how to feel what they ate—they chattered as they ate, always trying to guess where the gold might be, and did not realize that they were eating it. The wealth they were looking for was in the quinoa and the *morayas*, in the aroma of the *huacatay*, in the spicy flavor of the *uchukuta*, in the light that both the Sun and the cooks had deposited in the food. Paradoxically, our dear brothers would not have done too badly harvesting the spices our people used to elevate the tastes of our food since in Europe at that time, these types of spices were worth as much as silver and gold.

We made a mistake thinking that the conquistadors, after having enjoyed the powerful foods we offered them, would have felt satiated. That after filling their emptiness, they might have been able to relax. But when we realized that, like a bottomless barrel, they could never be filled, it was too late. After spending some days with our families, one night while we slept, they began to kill people and take the land that had produced what they had eaten. After killing many, to alleviate the heaviness in their souls, they violated our women and continued on, appropriating everything for themselves, forcing our men to work for them until their very bones broke. Victors in a war that they themselves had invented, they imported their Europe and laid it upon our lands, building a new world of towns with plazas, churches, and barracks.

Christopher Columbus never discovered this continent, nor did the conquistadors who followed, for they very quickly created a fiction called "America," a new, imaginary world to satisfy all their appetites and ambitions. Five hundred years have gone by, and still they are not satisfied. Conquistadors, some local, some foreigners, continue taking everything they can from our land and people without considering the life and beauty that they themselves, with all their capacities, could care for.

But we must also acknowledge, with gratitude, that something is changing for the better now and that we no longer have to hide in order to pray and make offerings to nourish our Mother Earth. More and more, people today are becoming interested in ancestral wisdom—from here, from Europe, and from the entire world. And when they feel well seen, the cultural treasures of our ancestors come out of their hiding places with all their beauty, their sacred power, and their ability to organize society. Now we can contemplate, as a valid alternative to the crises of our times, the contributions of the original culture of the Andean-Amazonian world. Our culture proposed, and still proposes, a way of life based on the fulfillment and satiety of the human being. In order to generate abundance and well-being, this way of life does not require individual ambition as a motor to fuel the progress of humanity. This peaceful cultural alternative wants the seeds that inhabitants of the past deposited in us, their descendants, to germinate in this moment of rebirth, the moment of starting over from the beginning.

In the beginning, the creators of our culture, recognizing how dangerous hungry people can be, drew on the power of food to develop a way of life that permitted our people to always feel full, satisfied, and grateful. Throughout this work,

I will show the sacred thoughts of our ancestors and how they demonstrate what I have just said.

To begin with, I propose that we investigate the real significance of the name of the founder of our culture in Lake Titiqaqa—the name *Manqo Qhapaq*. As is well known, in Quechua the meaning of "*Qhapaq*" is "principal," "rich," and "abundant." But there is no agreed-upon understanding of what the word "*Manqo*" means. Since we know that *Manqa* means "pot" (the container in which food is cooked), in my opinion, and in the opinions of people I have talked to in the communities in the Sacred Valley of Cusco, just as the words "*Wak'a*" and "*Wak'o*" have been used interchangeably to refer to the containers of something sacred, we have done the same with the words "*Manqa*" and "*Manqo*." Therefore, *Manqo Qhapaq* means "the main cooking pot," or "the main container, rich and abundant, in which food is cooked." We see within this meaning, assigned to the foundational principle of our culture in the area of the highlands around Lake Titiqaqa and the Sacred Valley of Cusco, the great importance our wise ancestors gave to the power of food. In addition, we will see later that our ancestors lived with an awareness that food produced by the Earth contains light and that they understood that their development into *Runa* (authentic human beings) depended on making sure that they possessed the greatest content of light possible inside their bodies.

Author's Note

◈

Our large territory in the Andean-Amazonian region is composed of forests, mountains, valleys, deserts, and oceans. Over a long period of time, we have learned how the land, the sources of food, and the spirits of each place influence the way that each community designs its culture. We are all the same in our essence, but not in form. We know there are many different worlds within our world, and the beauty of this diversity continues to amaze us. Therefore, as I share aspects of our culture that has expertise in the production of both material and spiritual nourishment, I do not expect that people who live in distant lands will adopt a way of being exactly like ours. However, there is something essential and universal that our ancestors cared for, and it could be useful to people throughout the world in this moment, when so many are seeking better lives and a way to continue living on this Earth.

I use the word "sacred" to refer to an energy that poses an elevated frequency of vibration that creates well-being for all and not in relation to any religion. When I refer to a real human being who recognizes herself or himself as a child of the Earth, I use the word "*Runa.*" The word "*Hallpa,*" I use to refer to the Earth as physical space. And I use the word "*Pachamama*" for Mother Time-Space, composed of all times, the four directions, and the three levels of existence (upper world, middle world, and underworld).

What I have written here was born from my experience of life and my way of interpreting our culture. I am not an anthropologist but rather a conductor of sacred ceremonies who has been instructed by elders who still preserve and use our ancestral traditions. While I have paid attention to the valuable contributions of other investigators of the Andean world, the principal method I have used to come to the understandings on which this work is based has been via the practice of the state of consciousness called *Yuyay* in Runasimi (the Quechua language), a state of being in which thinking, remembering, and understanding come to be the same.

In being faithful to this method of my Andean ancestors, I have not been able to be faithful to the European scientific method, which has not yet been able to recognize the existence of the spirit world. Therefore, I do not expect

the colonized society of the Americas to value my interpretations or to consider these writings an official source of
exact data concerning the culture of Indigenous communities.
Very simply, I have decided to reclaim the inheritance left
to us by our ancestors and, in my books, I make nourishing
offerings prepared with words—offerings in which I share
the treasures I have found while following a call, just as if I
were traveling along a path, following the song of a bird that
doesn't let herself be seen.

Arkan Lushwala

I OPEN MY MIND LIKE A FLOWER

AND LET THE BEES DO THEIR WORK.

I OPEN MY MIND FOR THE SUN TO ENTER

AND LEARN TO RECEIVE MY THOUGHTS.

I OPEN MY MIND LIKE A FLOWER,

AND LET THE HUMMINGBIRDS GATHER THE NECTAR.

I OPEN MY HEART SO THE EARTH MAY ENTER,

AND LIKE A BLIND MOLE BURROWING,

I FEEL THE PATHS I CANNOT SEE.

FIRST DOOR

❖

The Awakening of Our Will

1

THE WILL OF THE HEART

❖

We can all create our own well-being and that of those around us using the way of conscious will. The cosmic light that flows outside terrestrial space already possesses a very high vibrational frequency, and it is not up to us to alter it. However, we can utilize our will to influence the state of the energy that lives within our bodies and all earthly bodies, changing it in ways that make it more vibrant and that augment its beneficial power. By just pronouncing a good word, the will of our heart (*Munay*) may elevate the vibrational frequency of the energy and improve things in our surroundings. When we feel inspired, there is nothing that can stop us from bringing about actions that improve the lives of our people. We feel inspired to act because something moves us.

The will power, *Munay*, that we use to care for ourselves and the world does not come originally from us. In the beginning, it was light coming from the cosmos. We acquire it just by being members of a generous Universe that causes its power to circulate everywhere, making it available to all beings—large, medium, and small—without discrimination. Universal power makes itself available to us through the many ways in which it nourishes us. We receive nourishment from the light without condition simply because we belong to the Earth as part of the help that every creature needs to continue living and to develop their potential. One only needs to breathe deeply to receive energy, and no one receives a bill at the end of the month for breathing, neither the *Runa* who succeeds in going beyond their limits nor the beetle that moves a ball of earth ten times larger and heavier than itself nor the small bird that dances with all its enthusiasm to attract the female with whom he will have children.

Our culture, which has expertise in community organization, was designed in remote times to help us be conscious of belonging to the Earth and the Universe in such a way that each of us can have a direct relationship with the sources of energy that feed our will. Without this relationship, and without will, we could not develop ourselves as individuals with the capacity for supporting our community, our beloved world. Instead, we would allow others to take charge of our destiny, as happens in societies where children are taught that the most powerful men, some heroes and some villains, act as the main source of everything good and everything bad that happens in the world.

Munay awakens in our interior when we realize that the cosmic energy is always in front of our noses, and we learn to inhale light to benefit ourselves and to blow light to benefit others, participating in the circulation of sacred power that nourishes everyone. Breath is elevated to a sacred level thanks to a word we use to name it, the word "*Samay*," which, depending on the context in which we use it, can mean "to breathe," "breath," "to rest," or "to blow with purpose." The light we breathe that we call energy has already traveled through the starry world and crossed through the door of terrestrial space, where we live, in order to convert itself into the vitality of nature and of our bodies. This universal food, although it is everywhere and accessible to all, must be harvested and taken with determination. To be the masters of our own well-being, it is indispensable that we pay attention to the quantity and quality of nourishment we take in from the source because, like all energy, our *Munay* can be either abundant or deficient. The food we take in determines whether our will grows—whether it acquires the power to make us want to participate in the dance of life—or whether it becomes paralyzed like something isolated and useless. With a strong *Munay* in the heart, any individual can, in any given moment, elevate the light stored within to high frequencies of vibration, making possible the impossible, overcoming their limitations.

It brings us great benefit to grow our internal content, receiving food from above, from the middle, and from below. The food from above (*Hanaq Pacha*), all light born in the sky, feeds us through our eyes, our skin, and our breath. Getting up early to greet the first rays of the Sun, we receive great quantities of this food that, in addition to giving us vital life force and health, also helps our body remain well-informed and up-to-date, like a body that shares in what the Universe that it belongs to knows. The food we receive from the middle world (the surface of the earth, or *Kay Pacha*) comes to us from the heart of other *Runa*, from the affection of plants, animals, mountains, lakes, and many other creatures that share this earthly space with us. The light they radiate causes our hearts to vibrate, producing within us a song of gratitude in response to the help of those without whom we could not continue living. This light from the middle world, the light of sharing, keeps us awake by keeping us aware that we are all united and that we depend on one another. Finally, we receive light from the world below (below, or within, the surface of the Earth, called *Ukhu Pacha*), the light that vibrates in everything that emerges from the Earth that she gives us to eat. This light, captured in drops of water from dew, at dawn enters into the darkness of the Earth. It is also captured during the rest of the day by the green leaves of plants, which send the solar energy to the roots and soil. This light provides instructions to *Hallpamama* (the physical body of our *Pachamama*). These instructions come from her elders in the Universe (the stars), who fulfill their mission of helping her know how to continue developing as a living, cosmic being. And each time we eat something natural, the instructions given to the Earth are transferred to our bodies, favoring our physical, mental, and spiritual growth. These instructions, essential to Earth people, help us adapt to an ever-changing natural world.

❖

In a wise democracy of our ancestral type, everyone must have the same access to these nourishing practices that make the content of light in our body and our spirit grow. Everyone must be able to count on the energy needed to increase our *Munay* in a way that we can collaborate in conditions of equality, uniting our forces so as to resolve the problems we have in common. To accomplish something together, we all need to have sufficient *Munay*, and a *Munay* that has been instructed, informed, and guided by the Earth and the Universe. With abundant *Munay* we are able to open the paths that favor our health and happiness, and without *Munay* we could end up converted into people disconnected from source, unmotivated, and who can easily be manipulated.

While it would be ideal for the majority of people in a community to have will, it is not demanded of anyone that they mature with excessive hurry. We *Runa* take our time to grow just as plants do, and not everyone grows at the same rate as another. The *Runa* who take it upon themselves to receive nourishment, so as to be able to give nourishment, begin their development in infancy and need many years to complete their growth. We need to be patient with others, even when it is urgent—today more than ever—to be assured of having mature people in our communities.

2

A Type of Indigenous Democracy

❖

As a form of reciprocity, we farmers contribute something to the Earth that feeds us. Something marvelous happens when the light from the sky, which enters edible plants, is combined with the tender care we express while helping them to grow. We speak to them from the time they are seeds, praying for them to become large and healthy, and the light that leaves our mouths gives them the encouragement and the power (*Kallpa*) to develop well. After a short time, the consecrated plant feeds us and comes to have great influence over our affectionate way of being. From within, the plants that we cultivate and eat guide our will and motivate us to maintain our health and to live in a healthy, undamaged world.

For our ancestors, the will to live in a healthy, undamaged world became the origin of their form of social organization. The world in which we live needs to be constantly restored.

Well-being requires maintenance, and natural disasters need to be prevented and attended to. From within, Mother Earth guides us so that we know how to restore our world and calls us to organize ourselves as a people united and in permanent communication with her. By listening to what moves us from the natural world, we can all, with our own talents, influence the quality of life of our families and of our lands with the same power as those in official positions. We are well organized when all the members of our community (or nation) use their will, on a daily basis, to generate actions that improve our territories and the quality of our lives. Democracy does not mean giving power to others so that they can do for us what they alone decide. It means participating daily in the activities that form our world. Listening to nature with our bare feet touching the Earth, breathing in the scent of the mountains, paying attention to the feelings that arise spontaneously in our hearts, we become aware of decisions that we need to make without delay. Flowing with the calls of nature, we take care of whatever is needed in the moment while noticing what works best in a particular environment at a particular time. And we call the women and men who live in this way *Runa*. The *Munay* of the *Runa* gives life to the kind of social organization in which we all generate solutions to our problems, full of inspiration—and by inspiration, I mean inhaling wisdom from within so that this wisdom provides determination and direction for our actions.

In the Andean-Amazonian world, that which I call "democracy" has been a natural practice since the time of our ancestors, a practice born from the hearts of people who respect and make use of the complementary differences that exist among people. Complementarity has the power to sustain community life, making it inclusive and caring, enriched by all the good relationships on which the production of good food and an affectionate social environment depend. But we not only need to care for the relationships between us humans. In the Andean-Amazonian world, we also consider our relationship with the Earth as crucial, and the same care applies to our relationship with all the beings in the natural world, including the stars that shine down on us. In order to be in good relationship with the natural world, we must communicate with beings who are not human, something rather difficult for people in the modern world to understand but essential in Indigenous cultures.

When our white relatives from Europe came here for the first time, they could not understand, nor even conceive of the possibility, that there existed societies, such as we had in our villages, that did not obey a centralized power of human origin like the kings, bishops, and generals that they obeyed in Europe. This explains why the first chroniclers assigned to write about our culture constructed an imperialist image of the so-called Incan Empire, similar to the form of government that existed in European kingdoms at the time. They didn't know how to conceive of something different. Only in recent years have researchers such as Franklin Pease proposed that the "*curacas*" (chiefs later called caciques by the Spanish authorities), who served as leaders in Andean-Amazonian human groups, were not assigned to their posts by the ruling *Inka* and therefore did not belong to a hierarchy of pyramidal authority. The *curacas* were not people entrusted with authority by the *Inka* but rather by the people of the communities they belonged to. Consecrated to their posts in a ritual manner, they had to demonstrate that they had the trust of the great spirits of nature in the area where they lived and that they knew how to listen to them and feed them well.

In terms of intercultural relations, very little has changed in five hundred years. The gap that exists between our culture and cultures of European origin continues to be a very large one. The relationship between the Indigenous communities on our continent and the colonized states in which their territories are located has never been good, and that must be, in part, because we do not understand each other. Why is it so difficult to understand that the Indigenous give more importance to protecting life than to defending an ideology or a specific political or economic model? No matter what political party is in power, there is another power that guides us, calling for our attention. The life of nature always requires attention. Listening to what the spirits of nature tell us influences our decisions. The influence of the sacred power that organizes the Universe and nature extends into our human communities, our homes, and our workplaces. Perhaps we will understand each other better when the modern world accepts this sacred, universal influence and allows it to impact every part of society, including governments and the authorities who make decisions that affect the lives of all.

Neither plants nor animals nor the natural world know anything about political ideologies or scientific predictions, but they are able to immediately detect the presence of anything that threatens their health, their equilibrium, or their continued existence. Being in such close contact with the natural world, we *Runa* also share this capacity—the capacity to sense and to feel. According to Indigenous understanding, the scars that human activities leave on the Earth can be healed or can be used to create beauty, but our actions can never be allowed to permanently damage the balance of nature. When neglect causes us to abandon the one who gives us life and food, whether it is our biological mother or Mother Earth, we feel danger, and we know that soon our own destruction will come.

It is difficult for me to understand how there exist

authorities who want to govern without taking into account the truth of what is happening to Mother Earth. She supports their own life as much as ours. It makes me dizzy, listening to them talk back and forth with their own ideas—endless ideas about how things might be going and what living beings might need—without being interested in listening directly to those living beings who know so clearly what they need. It is difficult for me to understand systems of government that pretend to care for communities without considering the health of the actual environment of those communities. It is difficult for me to understand societies built on accumulation of damaged relationships and to see the constant discussions that take place in democracies, the fighting between candidates and elected officials, and the way they are unable to work together for the common good. And above all, it is difficult for me to understand how no consideration is given to the extremely dangerous situation that results from this damaged relationship between human societies and Mother Earth. Without a doubt, we are being governed by a political system without *Munay*, with little intelligence, and which is so poorly developed that it cannot receive instruction from the Earth and the Universe. Because of this, our political system possesses the tragic ability of leaving its people always unhappy and unprotected.

3

THE DESIRE TO LIVE

◈

In Quechua, to say "liberated" or "free" one says *Q'espisqa Kay*, which also means "to be crystalized." The crystalized *Runa* know how to use *Munay* to achieve their aims, especially when their aims are related to the common good. In a sane world in which the culture supports the crystalization of individuals and communities, people live content and in good health. When big problems arise, acts of solidarity produce joy in their hearts. Such acts abound in a world full of truly mature people, in a society based on communitarian life. In such a world, people do not shrink from their fears. In such a world, fear of death does not really exist since a fulfilling life has a great chance of ending with a peaceful death. But this world, in which human societies enjoy the same vitality, joy, and enchantment that nature has, now finds itself interrupted. This is the world that we lived in before the European colonizers came.

Now people live in fear. To feel interrupted, without naturally flowing and without a great desire to live, has become common. Both for us and for Mother Earth, who feels our steps and our heaviness—it hurts to exist this way for such a long time. Before the interruption, we cared for the world by nourishing the sacred every day, and sickness and lack were kept at a distance. The sacred sources that fed our inner content infused us with the desire to be joyful, to create, to reproduce, and to make our communitarian homes beautiful. But today, suffering tremendous stress, hurried and without the time to rest and feel nature, some of our people no longer have the capacity to store sufficient light inside themselves. Nearly everyone has traumas and open wounds through which they are constantly losing energy. To compensate for the loss of well-being, many of them consume too much sugar, alcohol, and flour. Obsessive thoughts and emotional crises cause them to act in self-destructive ways and in ways that are destructive to their closest relationships. Any individual who doesn't know how to fill themselves with light to increase the quality of what lives within them—their energetic content—might come to an extreme state, feeling that life has no purpose, and temporarily lose the desire to live.

The desire to live, enormous in those who possess a large content of light stored within themselves, makes these individuals exude an energy that nourishes all life. People like them naturally support the well-being and the continuity of life, both their own and everyone they touch with the energy of their presence. They do not seek a purpose for living because their purpose has already been clarified by the light within themselves. Their purpose is expressed through their desire to carry out work with the simple joy of helping other beings without the need for prizes or recognition. On the other hand, although they may remain busy and seem to be OK, those who lose the will to live are becoming ill.

Losing the will to live and the capacity for sharing life openly with others can cause illness. Self-medicating through toxic substances helps regain the will momentarily but over time only makes things worse. The best results come to those who decide to receive help from what they eat, from natural medicinal products, and from people who know how to heal others mentally, emotionally, and spiritually.

In the majority of cases, illness produced by the loss of the will to live begins to manifest itself in the mind, and one notices this observing one's own thoughts. When the thinking mind loses the will to support life, it becomes malicious and destructive. Then one must act quickly and take natural medicines that have been known about for a long time in Indigenous communities that help one to become calm and detoxify the destructive thoughts. Each ancestral community has its natural medicines and healers who have the knowledge to use them.

As long as one has even the slightest will to heal, they can heal themselves, and it is recommended to get help without delay so that their mental despondence does not fall, by its own weight, from the mind into the mood, creating a condition in which one can no longer be in good spirits. When it is already too late to heal the thoughts and their toxicity reaches the vital essence ("ánimo"), the vital essence is weakened, detaches from the body, and begins to wander, and one is no longer animated but is rather dispirited. Then one must take other kinds of medicines in order to be re-rooted in the body, such as spring water, minerals, and healing roots, or visit someone who has the gift of retrieving the vital essence (ánimo) of those who lose it.

People who have the gift of healing others can also perform "*Muray*," which means "to transmit energy to another to cause a change in their body," a necessary action when a person's discomforts that originate in the loss of their vital essence causes a split between the body and the spirit. What we in the Quechuan world see as the flight of the vital essence, or ánimo, our relatives, the Aimaras, see as *Lloq'empa*: a state produced by a misalignment of the spirit and the body, which healers perceive as the spirit detaching from the body, inclining leftward.

After reaching the soul, despondence can continue advancing and can reach the physical parts of the body. And if too much time goes by, one runs the risk of the body becoming disconnected from the sources that feed its vitality, of losing interest in living, and of no longer knowing how to receive and be guided by vital information that the intelligence of the Earth and the Universe provide. Sooner or later, the body's command center will cease giving the necessary life orders. On the contrary, it may give orders that slowly lead to self-elimination, generating extremely serious illnesses, like auto-immune diseases. When the loss of vitality reaches the physical body, the mind must still be healed and the vital essence recovered, and medicines must also be taken to restore physical health, identifying the internal organs and systems that were damaged. Medicinal plants have the ability of communicating to the body what it has forgotten, and when the body finally remembers its mission, it regains the will to live, increases its vitality, and can heal more quickly. Returning to being healthy and animated, reconnected to the source of the vitality of the Universe, life continues. Returning to the pulse of the heart of the Earth, the human heart recuperates, and the will for participating with others in the dance of life returns. One regains the desire to reinsert oneself into a family and a community, becoming like a tree in the forest that helps other trees grow while receiving from other trees the same help.

❖

In the long run, recovering the ancestral cultural wisdom that supports deep well-being can prevent so many from becoming sick, like what is happening today, but this will be the work of generations, and it has only just begun. In the meantime, we can learn to heal ourselves and stop small pains from turning themselves into serious illnesses. In Quechua, when we wish someone to be healed from illness, we say "*Hanpichikuy*," which means "make yourself healed with tenderness for your benefit." This shows that we understand the great importance of *Munay*, the will, in "making oneself healed." Those who want to heal take very determined initiatives that lead to healing since even when receiving the help of specialists, it is the owner of the body who decides to heal the body. Once, when having health problems, my wife, Marilyn, found herself in a sacred space she'd gone to receive help. There she was told: "When wild animals become domesticated, they get sick in their minds. They get sick because they no longer own their will and therefore become incapable of healing themselves when their problems are just beginning. You still have a part of yourself that has remained wild. Use it. Draw from it the will you are needing to take charge of your own life."

What Marilyn heard shows the close relationship that exists between self-care and having a strong *Munay* in the heart. To be able to take responsibility for our own lives, we need to commit to making our will grow. Then *Munay* needs to be respected as a natural power, fed by the sky and the Earth, that doesn't require human domestication—domestication diminishes its power. The "educational" efforts of colonialism, which tried to make Indigenous people "good Christians," adaptable to a Eurocentric society, was a form of domestication. And it put us in conflict with ourselves, with our own wild selves, with our natural tendencies, with our Indigenous mind, to the point of making us sick. As it is well known, in some towns along our continent where Indigenous people or their descendants live, there are serious problems of alcoholism, domestic violence, and other chronic diseases. With a good heart, some organizations that come to offer help do so by providing more domestication. In my humble opinion, we need to heal ourselves with the resources and medicines of our own cultures. With enough bravery, we may become as awake as a *Salqa* (wild *Runa*, like a jungle person) every time we need to listen, get in motion, survive, and grow with the adversities. To recover our space will be very helpful because the paths that lead us to becoming crystalized, as our ancestors did, are, for now, in the same condition they found Machu Picchu when it was rediscovered—intact but totally covered up.

4

RESTORING THE WORLD

❖

While enjoying good health, every *Runa* has the ability to restore the world. When facing the need to restore the world, we can make use of the talents inherent in our species, as people capable of transforming matter by creating change in its physical form, its chemical composition, or its vibrational frequency.

Our ancestors transformed rocks by cutting them and placing them together to build temples. They transformed plants by combining them to create powerful medicinal drinks. They converted the pigments and minerals of certain plants into paints for drawing the movement of sacred powers onto their faces. And without changing the visible form of a mountain or a lake, they were able to transform them through the simple act of elevating their vibrations by offering them a sacred name, a song, a dance, or the smoke from a gift of food and flowers given to a ceremonial fire. Water that came from the sky or was gathered from a spring was transformed into powerful medicine by inviting it to rest on stone altars and for the stars to shine on it at night. Similarly, they transformed the breath and water in their mouths into luminous powers that healed others through sacred speech or through a kiss.

The art of transforming matter—consecrating it and raising its vibration—causes the light that lives within it to acquire new forms and new powers. Then those spirits that we help form within things are converted into sacred sources that live with us in our houses and communities. They become allies that we can turn to when we need help to restore ourselves or the world. From remote times, in Indigenous communities, we have participated in the formation and growth of sacred spirits from whom we can ask help. We form them, and they form us. We elevate them, and they elevate us. Conversing with them with profound affection, we can go as far as to actually improve the climate and heal nature.

In order to restore the world, in addition to using the talents we have to transform matter, we also depend on powerful allies who hear us and want to help us, which only happens when we have cultivated a good relationship with them. In our thousands-of-years-old culture, it has become an art to express our gratitude, with flowers and tears, to the great powers of nature. The world becomes tired and hollowed out when we extract things from it and needs to be restored with frequency. We remember that everything we extract from a part of the land has its "owner," the guardian *Apu* of the area, and we always ask the owners for permission before doing our work. We feed them with an offering to compensate for their losses even before doing the work, filling in the holes that we will leave in their territory. Among the owners of certain territories, there are huge mountains. A mountain *Apu* (great mountain spirit), with its higher rocks pointed like antennae and a great belly for digesting enormous amounts of cosmic light, provides precious energy to us, and so we give much importance to our relationship with him or her. An *Apu*, not always a mountain, can also be a special spot in a forest or jungle, a powerful place in the desert, a star, the lightning, a constellation, or a divine being that guides us from the spirit world. We respect and nourish the *Apu*, regardless of its kind. And if through some carelessness we damage an *Apu* or its territory, we take measures to restore it immediately with the energy of a ritual.

With the power of our *Munay*, we know how to restore the world, feeding those who feed us. We do this through offerings, songs, dances, and with the sacred words that we use for making petitions. With this heart that we give them—our own heart—the *Apus* ("*Apukuna*") respond to us tenderly and take good care of us by increasing our energy, health, and good fortune. Most importantly, they allow us to harvest our food and to gather the materials we need to build our houses and to do all of our labors without breaking the balance of nature.

❖

In Quechua, we use the word "*Ayni*" to name the ancestral practice of feeding those who feed us. Without fear of being in error, I can affirm that *Ayni*, as a foundation stone, sustains the entire temple of our ancient culture. In modern culture, because of a mercantilist mentality, it has become common for *Ayni* to be misunderstood as a payment. But the true *Ayni* goes beyond giving one thing for another. The true *Ayni*, unlike payment or barter, manifests itself as a commitment that lasts over time. It requires a type of care, which moves us to quite literally "raise" anyone with whom we have a genuine interest in having a very good relationship. And we do this with the same care we raise our children with. Through beautiful gifts and attention, we also raise mountains, lakes, forests, brothers, sisters, and powerful sacred beings from whom we receive help.

At first glance, it might seem that the practice of *Ayni* and the custom of restoring the world through reciprocity belongs to a culture of people purely interested in their personal well-being. But in reality, the will that causes us to care for the sources of our well-being with great tenderness lacks selfish ambition. Rather, it is born from genuine affection and a deep desire to show gratitude. It would be very difficult to find in our culture people who contaminate their will by putting it at the service of greed. Such a level of ambition only appears when people forget the riches they already have, the wealth born of simple satisfactions. In our culture, wealth does not come from accumulating things but from having good relationships. We can fall into material and spiritual greed only if we lose pleasure in everything we have already cultivated and cared for, neglecting the relationships that make us feel well, both in times of abundance and times of scarcity.

We use the talent that has been given to us to transform the material world, motivated by a deep feeling and the need of offering our reciprocity (*Ayni*) only for the betterment of things, seeking to embellish them and elevate their sacred power. The unconditional generosity we receive when the Sun rises, when the rain comes, when we see our food emerging from the earth, and when we see our children healed of illness motivates us to be generous with the world and to take action to improve it. The ancestors, our teachers, acted from a motive of gratitude even when making their great works, marvelous creations that required enormous skill and the effort of generations. They did not build those works in order to put them up for sale or to receive a prize. For them, to construct something grand and powerful was the same as making a small sacred offering or to bring medicine as a gift for a loved one. And for whom, then, did they make great temples of stone? In part, they made them for us, to thank us for not forgetting them and for keeping the memory of their wisdom alive. And they also made them for the sacred powers of the Universe so they would have beautiful homes here on Earth.

5

Restoring the World with the Word

❖

Our ancestors consecrated all their relations and the elements of their environment through rituals and tender forms of speech. They developed the power of their words and utilized them to infuse sacred energy in everything they named. And they communicated in languages that are highly conductive: *Quechua, Muchik, Aimara, Pukina*. Like our ancestors, we still use some of these languages because of the ways they help us build phrases and sentences that can create an unfragmented world. The language itself has a sort of glue that prevents us from speaking in a way that creates separation. Furthermore, the tenderness and respect with which we name all beings helps us cultivate good relations with everyone, even the snake, the tiger, the storm, famine, or drought. In the case of the snake, to give an example, we can simply name it "*Mach-aqway*," which refers to a creature without legs, potentially poisonous. Or we could call it "*Amaru*," a word that also refers to a sacred energy that moves under the earth. It is our choice how we see the snake and how we name it. The way we speak determines whether the reality we live in makes us fearful or inhabitants of a magical and sacred world.

Quechua, currently one of the official languages of our country, continues to be spoken by millions of inhabitants of the Andean world who enjoy the opportunity of saying beautiful phrases such as "*Chay mikhunachata panachay qoykuway, ama hina kaychu,*" which means "Give me, with tenderness for your benefit, that little harvest (food), my little sister, don't be like that." And that's how people express themselves every day. And of course, you can also say something that means "Hey, pass me the food," but only when someone is very angry with the person they're talking to.

To give another example, I will share that some animals have alternative names that are used to call them with humility and affection, respecting their power, and treating them as part of the family. For example, in Cusco we call the condor "*Pablucha,*" which means "little Paul," and there are elders who would not feel good if they heard us call it something else.

These affectionate languages help us care for our relationships, and caring for our relationships assures the continuity of our existence. We know that disharmony and chaos always come to teach us lessons and that, after each storm, the time arrives to restore ourselves. With this sacred manner of speech, we reanimate the damaged beings and recreate our world. Raising speech to the level of the sacred, we invoke the presence of the highest vibration of all things, including powers of nature that we do not understand but nevertheless respect.

To speak in a sacred manner does not mean to worship. In our culture, we see the sacred beings of the spirit world as partners and allies. We don't worship them because we find no benefit in separating ourselves from the great spirits, putting them in some unreachable place. The health of the world requires that we stay close, in good relationship. Also, I believe that to worship those powers that we ourselves fashion and consecrate could make us ethnocentric. Falling into cultural narcissism would lead us to assume that by having powerful gods we are better than the people of other nations. That would be a misuse of the precious brilliance of our allies that would lead to their deterioration. Therefore, we take great care to hold tender affection and respect for all the beings we have consecrated but without worshipping them or seeing them as if they were something perfect. The elevation of our culture does not require seeking perfection; it only requires that the gestures we make to attract the sacred be born from a humble heart.

The sacred word, like a magic key, opens every door, including those of the spirit world where there are wombs charged with potential, ready to respond to our songs and to give birth to that which we ask for in a good way. Fortunately, the human heart knows how to delight the spirit world, attracting it to ourselves, inviting it to move into the material world. And in this way we can restore anything we unfortunately mistreat when carrying out our productive activities.

SECOND DOOR

❖

The Place
Where Sacred
Rituals Begin

6

DEEP RITUAL

❖

In Indigenous communities, we always want to have clear communication, simple and profound, even when just making jokes. For this, we often use plants that facilitate the fluidity of our speech when we pray to the sources of our well-being and when we let expressions of affection directed to our relatives come to the surface. These simple rituals of the heart keep us healthy through our communication.

Those who speak with sincerity unblock themselves, and then energy can move more fluidly within them. Good communication does not require too much speaking. Words have more power when we do not abuse them and when we speak about things at the right moment. Words appear with all their power, beauty, and truth in special moments, for which we must wait calmly, sacred moments that appear when we listen and feel in silence. Without doubt, the right words, loving and luminous, come more easily with the help of sacred plants. They convert our breath and the water in our mouths into medicine. We use plants that spend their existence communicating with the Sun, that have the power to clear the channels through which the energy in our bodies flows. We receive and pass along energy through these same channels when we relate with other beings. In the Andes, the sacred coca leaf, *Kukamama*, has always helped us, while other Indigenous communities on our continent use ceremonial tobacco, cacao, red willow bark, guayusa, and yerba mate among other plants. In Asian countries, according to what I have heard, they have used tea leaves from the earliest days, and a woman from Ethiopia once told me that in her community they know how to conduct ceremonies for drinking coffee.

The experience of many Indigenous communities shows that the habit of taking a pause from work from time to time to enjoy these plants and to share a good moment with our fellow workers results in more productivity than the habit of working without stopping, because if we become ill we become less productive. In communities and groups of workers who don't take time to talk from their hearts, conflicts can sometimes remain alive and unresolved for years. To correct such defects in communication, these plants can be very helpful. Using them almost daily creates a custom of relaxing the tongue and allowing the expression of feeling to arise.

In cases where something too difficult has occurred and communication has become distorted—or where one cuts oneself off from a family member, community, or group of workers—in addition to using the plants mentioned earlier, it is important to conduct rituals of a high vibrational frequency. And it is highly recommended to do them without delay to avoid the burden of our collective human problems from descending into our *Hallpa*, our lands, into the places we walk and plant our food. If contaminated by a collective illness, the land where we live will begin to lose its vitality, and the illness is followed by scarcity. In such a case, the rituals help us locate ourselves right between Heaven and Earth. From that place we invoke the sacred powers and invite them to unite so as to recreate the brilliance of our being. By means of the profound collective spiritual experiences called forth by these rituals, we receive help from sacred sources and succeed in renewing our energy. Receiving energy from a sacred source while being together, we let the dependence we have on each other rest for a moment. This dependence, necessary and inevitable, when out of balance causes conflicts that make us close the channels we use to exchange energy. Upon reopening the conduits of communication among the members of the community, we reawaken and strengthen the natural talents we have and what each one of us has to offer to the group. We beautify our lives together and become healthy thanks to our ability to listen to one another. Uninterrupted circulation of energy, in the form of fluid communication, helps maintain the health of the mind, spirit, and body of those who form any union of people, whether a couple, a family, a community, or a nation. When an interruption or disruption blocks the flow, well-conducted rituals have the power to cause our hearts to become open again, and we regain our capacity to express the truth we discover in our hearts with full respect—through prayer, a song, or some other expression of grief, anger, joy, gratitude, or profound affection.

In order to benefit from the most effective healing rituals, we need the help that comes from the powerful *Munay* of men and women—who in Cusco are called *Paq'o*, or *Pampamisayoq*, or *Altomisayoq*—who know how to invoke the *Apus*. They invoke the *Apus* that gave each person their character when they were born so that each person can be healed according to their original nature. During these rituals, when we come to feel nourished by the sacred—satiated, satisfied, and with open hearts—we cross an invisible door and enter into the depths. From such depths, we feel inspired to consecrate all our relationships. We recognize that each one of us, in accordance with our nature—whether from the human, natural, or spirit realm—has our own path and a particular way of walking it. Only when we meet in the deepest place of sacred rituals do all of our paths come together as one.

We look at one another and, without resistance, welcome the magic while noticing which direction our common well-being wants to continue flowing. In these marvelous moments of pure joy in which our paths join, anyone can take the path of another for a moment. A young man can become a jaguar, a man can turn into a woman, a woman can be a child, a child can speak like an ancient woman, an ancient woman can become a mountain, a mountain can become a condor, and singers, like a river, can take us on a journey through the colors that paint our dreams. With just a few drums, some rattles, and a beautiful dance, we can accomplish all this.

The sacred ceremonies that help open our hearts and minds, conducted at a high vibrational frequency, form an essential part of the original design of the way of life of an Indigenous community. They offer all the members of the community the opportunity to observe the state of their energetic content and the chance to ask for help in keeping it in a healthy, expansive state. In a good healing ceremony, we participants receive help to seal our open wounds and to repair our energy leaks. As a consequence, we end up feeling the increase of energy in our body. Feeling renewed, with more desire to live, the individuals that comprise the group have a chance to assume responsibility for themselves, now able to carry out the necessary changes and not fall again into some sort of ill life.

7

BLACK LIGHT

❖

Thanks to the sacred ceremonies that we have inherited from our ancestors, we continue turning toward an essential light that lives in the spirit world that here I call black light. Our ancestors not only fed themselves on the solar light deposited in the fruits of the Earth. They also fed themselves on black light, just as they had learned to do in their mothers' bellies. At night, black light brought them insightful dreams, and in healing rituals it lent them its sacred power. This must be why our ancestors observed both luminous constellations and dark constellations in the night sky as well as some that have a combination of light and dark parts, such as *Yakana* or *Qatachillay*, in which there are two stars that shine like the eyes of a llama whose body is depicted by a dark patch in the sky. They saw these black patches in the dark sky as doors to the spirit world, as sources of black light, wombs that gave birth to powerful spiritual food. And they knew how to receive the black light from these cosmic sources and from other sources, like when finding themselves inside a deep cave, in the underground part of a temple, or in any place with their eyes closed.

We expose ourselves to the spiritual power of the black light to receive instructions, visions, and other types of help. In our ceremonies, which often take place at night, after making the offerings and petitions to the sacred powers, we are shown the path toward the source of what we need to remain satiated and to feel at peace. In this case, being satiated does not depend on having enough food to eat but on satisfying other types of hunger, like spiritual hunger. Together with spiritual hunger comes the hunger to understand, the hunger of our universal being (which our human side cannot fully understand), and the hunger of mysterious parts of our interiors that we only feel when we dream. At times, we can even suffer a hunger that belongs to our ancestors, when they need us to remember them in order to heal some trauma that they died with, a trauma that could be interrupting their journey. Words and medicine from the wisest people on Earth are not always able to satisfy these hungers just mentioned, even less so when there are several hungers combined. Our most satiating, sacred nourishment is born from wombs full of black light that can be anywhere. They can be in a constellation of stars, in the origin of our galaxy, or closer to us in the depths of the jungle or a mountain—even in some powerful stones. Therefore, in Indigenous communities we rely not only on the talents of our healers but also on the traditional sacred doors and altars that they open, through which the powers of the spirit world come to us to help us.

For Indigenous people, it has always been important to identify sources of black light and to have a good relationship with them, a relationship of mutual care. And this aspect of our cultures, rooted in ancient times, makes us always return to have meetings with the essential, ensuring that we do not starve spiritually. Ancient wisdom makes it possible for me to believe, without doubt, that we could reduce the amount of productive activities—ultimately unproductive because of the great harm they do to nature and vulnerable people—born from chronically unsatisfied people who always want more. We could do this by creating a world populated by physically and spiritually full, satiated people. In the Andean-Amazonian world, we know this from experience. We know that we can aspire to the building of a truly healthy world because we have done it before. We have done it without money, and with sufficient food for all—not only food harvested thanks to our knowledge of the predictable, but also spiritual food gathered by fishing the waters of the unpredictable, when we are guided by songs of the night, attentive to the generosity of the sacred powers of the Universe.

My ancestral grandmothers learned from the owl. They knew how to see black light where others saw only darkness, and they enjoyed the night. Then our European relatives came with their fears and taught us to be afraid of the owl. From religious motives (or from not wanting to lose control over the unpredictable side of nature) our ceremonies were not acceptable to the colonizers. In fact, they were prohibited, with claims that our ancestors worked with dark forces. But to work with the darkness does not mean working with dark forces understood as evil spirits. Very different from our own culture, the culture originating in Europe tends to associate the color black with the evil that is hidden in deceit, with darkness used in occult practices, and with the sorrow that follows a death. For some, a white cat crossing their path has no significance, but a black cat can cause fear and the worry that something bad is about to happen. Everyone loves white sheep, black ones not so much. So, with no intention of disrespecting our European relatives, I need to say that those who associate the color black with danger run the risk of forgetting how protected we felt when we were in the dark bellies of our mothers, forming our little bodies. And could it be that, in that sacred dark space that expanded within our mothers' bodies, we received something more than solely what she ate and shared with us but also some universal instruction, some essential spark necessary to growing into being? And could it be that after being born, we do not stop growing and so still need that food to keep our being alive?

The ancients lived trying to not forget the essential, that which they knew for the first time in the dark belly of their mothers. They were very careful not to use the darkness as a place full of forgotten things or like a cellar that stores hidden secrets, shameful memories, and old demons. Instead, they perfumed the darkness with incense and sacred plants to keep it clean and clear so it could shelter light we cannot see: the light of the parallel world, of the world-womb where everything begins to exist before it appears in the material world.

❖

When we speak about black light, right away it changes into white light, bright and visible. Because of this, unless we are in a sacred ceremony or called to transmit an ancient teaching, we don't name it, we just let it stay black. We don't need to speak much about it; we only need to know where to find it or how to make it find us. Leaders of sacred ceremonies learn to create spaces where silence finds those asking for help. In these spaces, black light finds a way to filter through cracks that powerful sacred rituals can open in their minds, beyond the usual human "clarity" that often keeps them blind. Truth and clarity do not always go together. Clarity's brightness may blind us and impede us from finding what hides in our depths, in the far territory of the forgotten. Too much mental clarity may also cause us to lose connection with the profound presence of the essential, a loss that could produce an abyss in the self—an incomprehensible anxiety that could make us overconsume in order to try to fill the void—leading us to take more from the world and our people than what we really need, causing tremendous harm.

8

Spiritual Work
to Heal the Earth

❖

Human greed has greatly damaged nature, and now we are
facing serious problems that have us worried. Those of us
who live in constant contact with the forms of life that live
in our territories—and with the water, wind, cold, and heat
that visits us—can see firsthand what is really going on in
nature. And we have very good friends who have studied in
good universities, who deeply love the Earth, and want to
help heal the damage we are seeing. And while we are very
grateful for what they teach us, at times we cannot understand why they trust so much in the knowledge they have
in their heads while forgetting to trust what the spirit of the
Earth says to their hearts, and even the healing power that
emanates from their own hearts.

When it comes to healing our territories, receiving wisdom from the spirit world becomes indispensable. We give

much importance to the exact date, place, and time in which we find ourselves when we begin such work because there are times and places where the border line between the material world and the spirit world becomes very thin. In those moments and places, it becomes much easier to cross. Wanting to come directly to the spirit of what we need to heal, we choose one of the places of power that exist in our territories and do the work from there. But it isn't only in our territories that we need to find places of power; we also have to find them within ourselves. We have many places within ourselves from which we can connect to the world, and when we need to connect to the spirit world, our hearts stand out like a mountain.

The heart has immense power since it serves as the place that receives our spirit in the body and makes a nest for it to repose. When body and spirit come together in the heart, they combine their energies and generate growth in our being and growth in our human capacities. When there are emergencies, something in the heart responds. Something powerful and sacred emerges from the heart—that is how emergencies help us. But what of the thinking mind? It can also help, but it does not have the same power. The thinking mind—which contemporary humanity mistakenly elevates above the heart—far from being a place of power, serves as a good tool for processing and integrating information. At times, it can be our worst obstacle. In support of our awareness, the mind needs to be humble, listening while thinking, listening to the little bird that lives in the heart and never stops singing. Awareness comes from listening to the heart in order to hear that which the spirit knows. To be truly intelligent we must decipher what the little bird says. And to accurately perceive what happens in nature, we must do so through feeling, like the jaguar who hears everything that is happening in the jungle through the soles of his paws.

Another power of the heart relates to dreaming. Our heart keeps alive the memory of the gifts we receive in our dreams that, upon waking, quickly leave the thinking mind. The heart does not forget what we find out (thanks to dreams) that we really want or truly know. During the day, in the middle of our activities, the heart sends signals to the mind to help it remember that we are also spirits that possess wisdom and have a sense of direction. And this helps our spiritual aspirations show up in those moments in which we choose our course of action. To remember ourselves as spirits, we just need to return to the place of sacred power at the center of the heart and be open to the feeling that comes. We meet ourselves here and also the light that came to nest in us. From this sacred place, we produce acts that heal the world, acts that result from combining our spiritual power with our human abilities.

❖

In the ancestral Andean-Amazonian world of which we are inheritors and apprentices, material development improved over thousands of years, generation after generation. People were accustomed to living with joy, harvesting the fruits of the Earth on the basis of their intelligence and industriousness and without forgetting that human intelligence has its limitations. When they needed to create a profound transformation in the physical material world, they first did so in the spirit world. Bestowing humility on their human intelligence, they created ceremonies in which they thought with their hearts, and they received visions that contained instructions and wisdom derived from the spirit world. Their great works, still admired today, were done not only through human intelligence but also with spiritual wisdom.

Some of us who are from the Andes or from Amazonia follow the custom of connecting ourselves with the spirit world before doing any work in the material world, just as our ancestors did. The spirit world is composed of the spirits of all things and beings. Some live very near us, and others live in very elevated or very deep places. Any work we do with a spirit, even something simple like bringing it an offering or making it vibrate with the help of a sound, will make that spirit increase its power. For example, if we learn to raise the vibration of a stone to the level of the sacred, that stone will be converted into medicine that can help heal others. To give another example, if we raise the vibration of a sick tree, that tree could have the power to heal itself. Because a spirit, when empowered by elevating its vibration, can transform the physical body that contains it or can radiate its power outward to help others.

Those of us who do sacred ceremonial work must introduce ourselves by name so that the spirit world, which already knows us, may remember us. And then, with permission, we can start making the requests, petitions, and songs that elevate the energetic vibration of all things.

For the *Paq'o*, *Pampamisayoq*, *Altomisayoq*, *Maestros*, or *Curanderos* as we are called in the Andes, it sometimes requires a lot of work, and other times very little, to make the black light, the spiritual content, raise its power and transform from within the body that contains it. It all depends on how we speak to the spirits that live inside things, on the way we sing to them, and on our ability to touch their hearts.

The examples I offered, that of the stone and the tree, refer to very simple situations. Something more complex and very beautiful happens when, beyond focusing on one specific being, we sing to the entire spirit world, sometimes even reaching the stars. Sometimes even moved to tears, we realize that the Great Sacred Power has heard us and given its attention to we very small beings that sing from our hearts.

And the song that follows arrives delivered to our mouths by that same sacred power, and immediately all within us and around us becomes the song, a universal song. And that vibrational power, that beauty with no specific origin, takes over and smoothly does the rest of the work. In the end, it decides what will happen, how far the healing can go. Sometimes miraculous things happen instantly, and at other times we realize that it was not the moment, that something wasn't ready, in which case the ceremony serves as a good step toward a goal that is still a little far off.

We can all learn to pray. Each of us has the capacity and the right to influence the state of the world using our spiritual power. There are those who have a gift and those who have been instructed by wise teachers, but anyone with a strong heart can command the health of other living beings to a certain degree. Those of us who dedicate ourselves to doing this work regularly respect the physical laws that keep life in balance every time we interact with the natural elements of the material world. And once we pass to the spiritual side, we seek to accomplish the impossible. Knowing the paths that lead to the spirit world, we visit it frequently. From there, we retrieve the wisdom necessary to heal illness and the loss of equilibrium in the material world. In original Indigenous communities, there are those who say that to generate the existence of something new or some change in the material world, we have to first create it in the spirit world. As my brother Manari—a son of the mother-jungle from the *Sapara* tribe in the Amazon Forest in Ecuador—says, "What is created in the spirit world manifests itself in the material world, and what is created in the material world manifests itself in the spirit world." Manari and the people of his tribe also say that to remember our dreams upon waking helps us very much because while we dream, the thinking mind relaxes and stops trying to govern. While sleeping, our ability to receive visions from the spirit world is momentarily restored, and we become capable of receiving insights and keys to understanding life situations that we normally do not understand. This ability has proven to be very helpful to us when working toward the healing of Mother Earth.

9

WAK'AS AND APUS

❖

At times, those of us who work for *Pachamama* by lighting sacred fires and singing to the *Apus* have the good fortune of finding or receiving stones and small statues that help us in our work. Some of these small stones and statues are called *Khuya*, and others are called *Illa*. This last word means light. And why was a little magic stone called "light" by our ancestors? Most probably they called it that in reference to the black light that lives inside them, the light of their dark wombs that we know how to impregnate with our prayers. Once we put our breath inside them, all that originates from our relationship with *Illas* and *Khuyas* must be considered our creation and our responsibility. Like our children, when the spirits that live inside these stones and statues begin to grow, they learn to speak in their own way, and we must know how to listen to them.

The ancients also called some of them *Wak'a* or *Wak'o*, and we still use those names today for a variety of things that serve to shelter and contain sacred energy. Our ancestors used the word "*Wak'a*" for buildings with sacred uses and also for places in nature where spirits live and speak, for rocks, sacred trees, wooden staffs, small or large statues, as well as for certain weavings and ceramics that were infused with sacred power. It is also known that in ancient times there were men and women of flesh and blood who were called *Wak'a Willaq* ("the one who tells what the *Wak'a* speaks"), or they simply used to call them *Wak'a* or *Wak'o* to describe their profession.

"*Waq'a*" in Quechua means "insane," and the slight difference between the sound of "*Wak'a*" and "*Waq'a*" makes me think that there is a connection between these two words, reminding us that insanity was a sacred profession in the time of our ancestors. It was required for providing certain types of spiritual service. It used to be seen as a positive quality because those who possessed it were more easily able to free their minds from the limitations produced by rigid cultural norms in order to go beyond what their society considered to be acceptable, possible, and real. In a few words, one must be "insane" to speak with spirits, and our ancestors had the humility and the wisdom required to accept and include those who possessed this gift in their social order. And they did not let themselves be deceived. They used great seriousness and discipline to distinguish real *Wak'as* from false *Wak'as*. Elders with experience knew how to detect whether there was really a spirit speaking through the mouth of a human *Wak'a* or not.

In the sacred world of my ancestors, they could tell a real *Wak'a* from a fake one. When they were stone, ceramic, wood, or a place in nature, the voices of real ones could be heard by the most developed elders, seers, and human *Wak'as*. As unbelievable as it seems, a true *Wak'a* says hello and calls out when needing to communicate something important. It knows how to answer questions and, above all, helps us understand things from the perspective of the spirit world, something necessary when our perception and intelligence turn out to be insufficient.

The *Wak'as* come to be diplomats to whom we assign positions in the spirit world. They serve as trackers and messengers and are able to intercede or simply help us see what we cannot see. Their power resides in the facility with which they can cross from one world to the other or even live in both worlds. Their power is fed by us, from our world, with elements of our world and the high vibrations that our artistic talents produce. And when the *Wak'as* feel content with the food that we have given them, they lovingly follow our commands. In some communities, we have heard master healers (*Altomisayoq*) talk about the powerful little stones that help them as "my flock."

In the ancient world, before the conquistadors came, the *Wak'as* participated actively and frequently in the care of the people, in agricultural works, and in the government of society. Above all, they helped as counselors who oversaw important decisions made by the leaders, on whom the well-being of the people depended. They were so respected that when the *Inkas* expanded throughout the Andean-Amazonian territories, they always honored the *Wak'as* in the communities that they dominated militarily, making offerings and listening to them with respect.

The participation of different *Wak'as* was so common in the Andean-Amazonian world, and for so many centuries, that the people developed mechanisms to ensure the truth of their messages, trying to maintain their sacred work at the highest level possible. Given this, it was extremely counterproductive that the colonial authorities silenced our sages and revoked the powerful positions of the great Andean-Amazonian spiritual leaders, attempting to replace them with Catholic priests. Our culture remains the same, and we continue to consult with spirits and to use sacred instruments of power, but we no longer have the "great priests" calling deception by its name when necessary. We miss our wise elders who were able to instruct and guide the magicians who worked with the *Wak'as* so that they would not fall into abusing or misusing power. Sometimes hidden, sometimes in full view, there are some today who use spiritual power for low-level purposes, causing harm.

The forgetting of ancestral knowledge makes it now necessary that we have to exert ourselves to distinguish between a *Wak'a* and an *Apu*. An *Apu* stands above us, and it does not owe us obedience even when it receives, like the *Wak'a*, the food we give it to demonstrate our gratitude or even when it owes the formation of its spiritual identity, in part, to us. The *Wak'a*, on the other hand, becomes our creation. Though we are not the creators of its prime material (some form of energy belonging to a natural being like an animal, rock, or plant), we do participate in the design of its form and give it its character. Therefore, we can reprimand *Wak'as* when they do not do their jobs well, as is sometimes done in communities that punish an ancient cross that has been placed on a hill. The cross is dressed, given offerings, and asked with sacred speech not to let hail fall on the crops. And if the cross does not fulfill its mission and allows a storm to destroy the crops, the people punish the cross with lashes. We can do this to a cross or some other *Wak'a*, but we would never do this to an *Apu*. The *Apus* (*Apukuna* in Quechua) remind us that our power is always under theirs. Very sacred and elevated beings who existed before us, the *Apus* help us be humble, and they balance us when we aggrandize ourselves and begin to do damage to nature with excessive will. There are ancient tales that speak about communities of very powerful people who, not wanting to obey, went to war with the *Apus*. In those stories the humans always end up losing and being sent to live underground.

The *Wak'as* help us work and achieve our purposes, enjoying the good life in the magical and surprising world that we consider our own. The *Apus*, on the other hand, have spirits from other worlds. They live in time frames much longer than ours and do not share in the pressure or sense of urgency that affects us. Therefore, to listen to an *Apu* requires a different level of attention that makes it possible to get a glimpse of reality from their perspective. To listen to the *Apus* requires us to be in a place deep within our own being, free of desires, a sacred place that needs to be clean and without interference so that we can receive instructions. The wisest men and women who guided our communities were people who spent their lives cultivating such a place within themselves and, in so doing, knew how to encourage others to do the same, elevating the culture of our communities.

They taught us that such an elevation of being happens each time we consciously expose ourselves to a vibration of a very high frequency that makes us feel at peace, and so we know to appreciate receiving the energy of the silent, powerful *Apus* that live near our communities. Our ancestors taught us to receive help from these sacred sources, and they also taught us that we must help ourselves. To elevate ourselves, we use our internal power and call our hearts to guide our actions. Thanks to the high elevations where the Apus who call us reside, we feel inspired to do the work to develop our highest potential. Becoming elevated can be a gift, a sublime experience that brings us to magical moments and places without having to make much effort. But if one wishes to repeat the experience many times at will, this requires persevering in the learning. Some efforts may be small, such as by smudging oneself with a sacred plant, and others require that we really stretch ourselves, such as when we need to stop our distraction, get focused, and change our attitudes.

The uncomfortable feeling produced by remaining at a low spiritual level for a long time continues growing within us unless we do something to get out of it. Once we leave that heavy feeling, we find ourselves at peace again, regaining our fluidity, feeling the Sun return to our smile, and recovering a sense of well-being. Oscillating back and forth, from forgetfulness to the recovery of an optimal spiritual level, we do a workout that leads to the growth of the most profound manifestation of our *Munay*—our sacred personal power.

❖

In the old days, teachings like this were ingrained in our culture. This remains so today but less than before. I hope we don't forget this. If we only see ourselves as physical beings, living in a material world, we will stop growing when our body stops growing, and then we may think that our well-being and security will depend on increasing our material wealth. But such successes will not bring an end to feelings of dissatisfaction, nor will we be able to avoid suffering, old age, and death. A good relationship with sacred spiritual beings, such as *Wak'as* and *Apus*, on the other hand, helps us remember our own spiritual nature, that we, too, are spirits in permanent need of growth. Then we are welcome to participate in the wonderful happenings of the spirit world, taking great care to attend to our need to elevate our spirits and to have our spiritual presence fully alive when met by another being.

10

CREATORS OF SPIRITS

❖

During the past five hundred years, we have hidden some things to protect them. We knew, without anyone telling us, what not to say in public. It was surprising to me when my good brother from the Ecuadorian jungle, Manari Ushigua, said in a meeting with people from several countries that we, the *Runa*, are creators of spirits. Since then, I have been grateful because I felt some sort of liberation. It became easier for me to share in public these kinds of profound spiritual themes that come from our ancient cultures.

I want to begin by clarifying that we, the *Runa*, do not create all the spirits with whom we have relationships since every living being in nature has a spirit, and there are spirits that are much older than humanity. The spirits that humans create are born from strong beliefs, grand ideas, visions, prayers, and collective devotional practices that make us constantly invoke their names.

That something becomes a spirit offers us many advantages since it enables us to have a dialogue in order to arrive at agreements that are mutually beneficial. In some places in the Andes, for example, hunger has been consecrated as a spirit. On the exact day of the first harvest of the year, it is customary in some communities to have a cheerful and colorful ceremony in which great offerings of food are given to the spirit of hunger. Having eaten, the spirit is accompanied to the border of the territory by the community, bid farewell, and commanded to stay far away until next year when the community has plenty of food to honor and feed it again.

In the case of illnesses that have come recently, such as the virus that caused the great world pandemic, we prefer to do everything possible to stop it from becoming a spirit. Most people I know tend to not give it a name or mention it by name. Although governmental authorities and the news said the name of the virus every day, we in the Sacred Valley of Cusco—while taking all the precautions suggested by the authorities so as not to become sick—only speak about "the flu." We do not have conversations that name or feed the presence of the virus, taking care to not turn the virus into a spirit that may want to remain living with us for a long time.

As creators of spirits, we have an enormous responsibility. Thoughts and feelings full of good intentions, expressed with words from the heart, consecrate kind spirits that help us, guide us, and protect us. And naturally this ability we have to create allied spirits has its polar opposite. With our energy dispersed, and without the guidance of *Munay* in our hearts, we can create spirits of a destructive type. Not everything that we plant in the spirit world ends up being sacred, and at times we create harmful spirits that enslave us. The energy of thoughts and emotions that express fear, jealousy, hatred, perversion, and greed creates spirits that are manipulative, jealous, and perverse. As humans, not knowing that we can do this with our energy would be like a bird not knowing it could fly or a fish not knowing it could breathe underwater. Just as we can populate our world with sacred spiritual entities that are luminous and compassionate, we can also populate the world with dense forms of energy that end up becoming hungry and insatiable spirits who go about looking for the energy they need in order to evolve, behaving like poor creatures who steal food, and they can even steal lives.

Whatever we create in the spirit world ends up manifesting itself in the material world. This becomes particularly relevant now that we are seeking to improve the health of humanity. Big businesses with big names turn into entities, spirits that speak to people through advertising and popular culture. Their influence in the material world could be, in some cases, a great help in improving the economy and the well-being of people. Many of these spirits (brands) that live in the modern world were designed on a foundation of falsehood, so they always have the capacity to deceive people, creating false illusions of well-being that hide the damage they actually create. For example, instances where soda is presented as a source of happiness when in fact it can be quite damaging given the amount of sugar it contains. Or when a bank presents itself as a protector of people. What is more, since the spirits of these businesses constantly feed themselves in order to grow bigger, there is a danger that they will become giants, transforming their owners and managers into zombies, completely robbing them of their time and energy. When this happens, such people may develop an insatiable hunger, become egotists, and become quite dangerous for the rest of us. Similar to what I have heard my brother Manari say, there are corporations, ideologies, institutions, fashion styles, and other kinds of spirits created by humans that end up dominating humans. Enormous spirits that steal energy from those who have relationships with them, little by little, digging out a hollow place in the energy fields of the body, causing them to lose their vitality and transforming them into people as insatiable as they are. Such people begin to think and act like predators and sometimes even betray the ones they love.

There are spirits of this type that, fortunately, fail to grow sufficiently, and they can easily be transformed back into pure energy. But there are others that have been fed for so long that coexisting with them, thinking like them, and acting like them has become normal. All through its history, humanity has created powerful spirits that harm people, spirits related to racism, colonialism, ethnocentrism, corruption, and revenge. And those hungry spirits do not remain confined in history books, but they emerge daily to continue eating, repeating their harmful actions through contemporary people. There are people working in the Congresses of our Republics still defending, to the death, the interests of the colonizers that existed five hundred years ago. There are journalists, writers, and people of every profession who act in the same way. The original colonizers who thought of themselves as superior, and with the right to be masters of everything—even of people's wills—clearly speak through the mouths of some of these people today. There are families who, for generations, have enjoyed economic prosperity even while surrounded by people in humble conditions, many of them working as their servants or employees. And despite all their privilege, they suffer. They are not able to rest; they continue to struggle to conquer what has already been conquered. They resist changing for the well-being of others, and so they become new links in a chain of suffering that has already become too long and too heavy.

No matter our position in society, we each have a spiritual

inheritance that includes a sick component due to the disgraces of history. To undo these inherited spirits that influence our obsessions and our egotism requires work, and the work requires remembering that our obsessions are made of the thoughts and emotions that have emanated from our families for many generations. Although this energy cannot be destroyed, it can be transformed. And to transform our own demons, we must do the work of looking straight at them, recognizing them, and accepting them as our painful inheritance. Once we position ourselves as their legitimate owners, we can use the *Munay* of our hearts to provoke their total transformation.

In the end, we can thank our ancestors for their mistakes, from which we have much to learn. People with true knowledge learn that their fears or desires can cause them to mistakenly create dense and hungry spirits that will dominate their children. When seeing their ambitions grow, they remember that greed can lead them to create spirits too big and powerful, over which they will end up losing control. Therefore, people with wisdom prefer the wealth of a humble life.

❖

In the modern world, we often create spirits that end up playing with us, while the ancients felt the responsibility to increase their own abilities before trying to steer the world or to command other spirits. Well-focused, our ancestors were able to maneuver in the vast spirit world with elegance and without getting lost. They created only what they could manage and did not create spirits like the one in the story of Frankenstein, in which a scientist uses human parts to create a giant and loses control over him, a story that, in my opinion, predicted what is happening in the modern world, where things are being invented that come to dominate us.

Our ancestors had a power much greater than ours because they were aware that the main spirit that they needed to create was their own. And they dedicated themselves to this. They gave much importance to the consolidation of their own spirits, whom they needed to become in order to live with determination and wisdom in this world. They also knew that, in the end, they would need a consolidated spirit to inhabit the other world after their deaths.

The creation of our own spirit never ends. None of us can be considered a finished product. Being born does not mean we have completed the formation of our being. The more formed our being becomes, the better fed and more robust we make it, the greater our ability will be to avoid becoming puppets of what our own energy creates.

The work that we have been doing since ancestral times consists of developing the will needed to avoid feeding spirits that help us destroy ourselves and of giving abundant food to spirits that give us the strength to carry out our healthiest purposes. In ancient cultures in different parts of the world, much importance was given to tending relationships with spirits who were good allies (saints, deities, mythological beings, *Wak'as*). The well-being of communities depends on these relationships. The most elevated spirits become pillars that sustain the people and the culture itself because they help give life a sense of direction. They show us a path and help us better contend with the mysteries of life and death. When one of these spirits ends up being forgotten, the culture changes. When a new spirit is born, or an old one is revived, the culture changes as well. And this is how it must be. We often renew our spiritual alliances based on our discoveries and our aspirations. In this sense, the culture of each particular human group grows as the result of the ongoing effort its people make to create a healthy link between their spirit world and their material world.

11

THE END OF
HUMAN SUPREMACY

❖

In other times, when nature lost its balance, it asked us for help because it knew that the *Runa* had the skills to elevate the vibration of the spirits that live within all things. It did so through messengers. Spirits were heard talking in the *Wak'as* and in nature, and those who had the ability to listen to them became their messengers. For this type of gifted *Runa*, it was also common to cross the bridge between the worlds, arrive on the other side, and offer a tender gesture to some spirit they found that was not doing well, whether due to destructive events caused by human error or by some mysterious cosmic or telluric event. By following the instructions that they heard in the darkness of sacred spaces, they went on to help beings and natural spaces completely recover from their damage as often as was necessary.

Today the entire planet has been damaged. And I have

heard well-meaning engineers and economists say that the repair of the world will come from them, from the light of their minds, rather than from the dark womb of the Universe. It seems as though they think their intelligence can be the door from which the solution will emerge, as if they could be mothers. But the healing of the Earth will not come about due to the success of a few intelligent men because that would just be a new demonstration of the human supremacy that caused the damage in the first place. The healing of the world will be created through the cooperation of everyone who lives on Earth, from the smallest microscopic creatures to the fungi, plants, insects, tigers, whales, engineers, grandmothers, and even the rays of light that descend from the sky and enter the bodies of each one of us. The Earth knows how to heal the Earth better than anyone. Remembering to listen to all the beings of nature that are not only asking for help but also offering their wise medicine will be the long-awaited end of human supremacy.

White supremacy is slowly on its way toward disappearing because every day there are more and more of our white brothers and sisters who do not support this ideology. More difficult to eradicate will be the ideology of human supremacy. In recent years, white supremacy has been so often named and exposed that it can no longer go unnoticed. In some years, in order to continue existing, it has to camouflage itself. Shapeshifting into human supremacy, this new disrespectful relationship with nature has also manifested in the behavior of those who have been colonized. In order to adapt to the modern world and get a job, we have had to learn the destructive behaviors of those who touted their supremacy throughout history. Just like an illness received through contagion, human supremacy has become a pandemic. We have all been colonized. At first, Europeans were colonized by other Europeans, and like in the old legends, those bitten by a vampire become vampires. Today one does not need to have white skin to be in the driver's seat of an excavator that destroys a forest. The one who holds the chainsaw in their hands decides whether the tree lives or dies. And while the descendants of the wise Indigenous did not invent the chainsaw, we too use them.

We have been taught to be human supremacists, and we have grown up in a world that doesn't take into account the wisdom of our thousands-of-years-old Indigenous science. Our methods have not been validated in the universities nor in the schools our children are required to attend. We have become accustomed to the science and technology that has given humans the power to dominate the world without consulting with natural, wild, or spiritual beings.

It would be amazing if we humans could dislodge ourselves from the center of our world and let ourselves become engaged by something sacred, a powerful source radiating its vitality and intelligence toward us. With all of us sitting down, listening, and ready, something very sacred could emerge from the center and give us the wisdom we are praying for. Only after this could we use our wonderful human skills to influence a change in the painful state of the world. To heal our damaged material world, it will be necessary to access the power of the spirit world, and we come closest to the spirit world when we are dying. When we feel our life may no longer go on, we are being offered an opportunity. When illnesses or natural disasters hit us, we receive a jolt that can make us wake up. In the state of vulnerability that we are in when facing death, we can find hidden wisdom. But one who only sees the positive side of things and sees oneself as the one who always solves the problem loses the opportunity of receiving help from death—to wake up. To dare, once and for all, to see and reveal the truth of nature in the way a very sensitive artist does.

Though I would have preferred not to have gone to school when I was a child and spend years imprisoned in a room where they taught me things I did not choose to learn, I still feel grateful for some of the things I learned there. In particular, a good teacher told me about the work of Vincent van Gogh, a painter of undulating sparks and dancing photons that passed from his hand to the canvas with their spirits intact. His work was alive. His work showed us how nature has to penetrate our mind in order for us to be guided by it. In order to work for the Earth, we need to have a Van Gogh type of attention.

Like this true artist who respected light and did not impose the vain perfectionism of experts on the delicate magic of our world, we can cross—from a place of silence, observation, and deep feeling—to the other side, the source behind the veil. With great care, we could bring something from the other side back here. And if someone asked me to choose between an engineer and Van Gogh to solve the problems of the world, I would choose both! I wouldn't exclude the engineers, because they also have something to offer. And my respect would grow greatly for any engineer who would dare to work with him, the madman. If Van Gogh would have been born in an Indigenous culture, he would have been considered a holy man.

In our village, the last one up on the mountain, the dirt road ends, and an abundant silence in which the *leq'echu* bird sings fills the air. Here, at times, we also cry the way Van Gogh cried. Here, all the engineers that come receive food and are well treated since we know that they can help us have more water and more food. But it grieves us that most of the time they are in a hurry, that they want to help us without taking the time to know us, missing the chance to discover what we know thanks to the humility with which our eyes look upon the world. Thanks to having been humiliated, we know that human supremacy can only end one person at a time. It ends when someone is on their knees and receives help from beings of the spirit world, when someone lost is guided by a star, when someone asleep is awakened by a dream, and when nature speaks and shares sacred power with someone who is praying, willing to listen, and taking the time that it takes to do these things well.

The times are changing, and it has become urgent that human supremacy ends so that we may have the humility to let ourselves be guided.

What replaces human supremacy will be born from the black light. It will be born from this long night, from the intuition that seeks to sense when something approaches, from the wombs of women and of Mother Earth that are ready to give birth to new ways of living, and from the hearts of grandmothers who have been silent, concentrating and full of care like beasts in the wild, praying for us, asking that we be protected.

But who can protect us from ourselves? It is up to each individual to make the effort to heal themselves. There are many of us throughout the world who have rebelled against our own lethargy, who have decolonized our belief systems each time we have been awakened by buckets of cold water produced by our own conscience in moments of illumination. And so we have come to understand that the devil was created by humans and that hell only needs to be feared when one gets used to living in it. We have stopped believing in the superiority of those who won the wars, who continue looking at us from the tops of their monuments. We look again at the world like wild people, like Earth people, like pure beings that take from nature only what we need to eat, and the rest we care for with respect and reverence. Despite what news reports continue to say, we can no longer believe that social conflicts always have good guys and bad guys, forcing us to choose one or the other. Remembering that life is always born from the union of two different sources, we use our hearts to unite ourselves, to unite everything, each time they want to separate or distract us. We can no longer afford to be distracted. Otherwise, human supremacy will continue to damage nature, and soon we will destroy everything that remains.

BLUE LIGHT

❖

Something magical and powerful arises when the spirit of the stars meets with the spirit of the plants and the spirit of water, as we—full of silence, with our bodies open and willing—eat some green leaves, some potatoes, or take a sip of water. We receive the same benefit that all beings on Earth receive when invited to participate in the balance of the material world as animated by the spirit world. Our human community becomes harmoniously aligned with the greater community of the beings of nature and also with the community of the stars that show up to shine on our gatherings and councils just as they reflect in nighttime waters.

Any moment of daily life can be converted into ceremony even in the full light of day. The womb of the Universe can give birth at any moment, and we can take notice. We can feel the moment in which gifts from the spirit world arrive, and on rare occasions we can even see them, as when the black light crosses the veil and passes into the material world, becoming visible as tiny blue dots, flashes of blue, or undulating blue threads that appear for a fleeting moment. I don't give much importance to whether we actually see the lights or not, but what they do to us matters. They make us into a necklace, in which all the beads, though different from one another, become united. Each present being, in such a place and time, is pierced by a blue thread, and they all receive the same messages that cross from the spirit world into the material. They pass into our interiors without excluding anyone, and in this way we all receive the same information, information that guides our collective understanding and the decisions that we reach by consensus.

Most of the time, we receive the gifts of the spirit world when we are together chewing coca leaves, doing a ritual, or simply sitting in the middle of a field, eating potatoes and fava beans. In those moments, and only in those moments, we collectively feel a sense of grandeur because we go from being members of a community, citizens of a nation, and inheritors of a cultural lineage to being children of the Earth and members of the Great Universe. A state of expansion, free of limiting identities, allows us to partake of collective wisdom and consciousness with everyone and also with the beings of nature that are all around us. And if one of us becomes nervous, needs to make a joke, or needs to do something so as not to feel possessed by a sacred power that cannot be controlled, we see it as a sign that something very good is happening.

The unfolding of our collective lives—today called "the ecosystem," in which humans and many other forms of life participate—receives the influence of the universal light, charged with information, instruction, and guidance. Although we are all capable of being receptors of the instructions that the Universe sends, the light reflects best in water, and for that reason women—the natural owners of water—have a great capacity to express what they feel and to initiate social movements that generate changes and improvements in our collective lives. Those of us who are not women are not excluded from receiving gifts from the light, but I have noticed that we don't always know how to pay attention to what we feel or that we don't know how to express our feelings without our internal fire quickly burning up the essence of what we want to say.

In our Indigenous communities in the Sacred Valley of Cusco, when we make decisions by consensus, informal conversations first take place in the homes of families where one hears the voices of the women. They then become very formal conversations in the community councils, where the men come forward to make their speeches and present their positions, taking into account what they have heard from the women at home. After hearing many speeches, toward the end of our meetings, we usually experience the healthy flow of our Indigenous democracy when we all feel the arrival of the truth. As if to greet this important guest that has suddenly showed up, in a natural manner and without excessive debate, we arrive together at the same conclusion and the same decision. Those in opposition, and those who present other points of view, help us think with more depth and to consider the complexity of a particular situation. And they know, like everyone else, that when the group arrives at consensus, the only thing to do is to welcome the new spirit that has been born without interfering.

Even if we have been entrusted with a position of community or spiritual leadership, we all listen to the knowing in the heart of the people. In order to make decisions by consensus, none of us can be a closed bead blocking the thread of light. All of us in the group must offer our hearts openly and attentively, without becoming stubborn or competitive. Then the light can pass through us smoothly, making us into a diverse but united group. This universal light gives us the capacity to distinguish true from false and to see the path that flows naturally.

To make good decisions, our communities also depend on the words of individuals who have the ability to not be distracted when others, carried by their beautiful chaotic humanity, do not detect the truth that circulates in the air that we can feel and breathe. These types of leaders who do not lose their attention are identified from the time they are children as people who possess a natural gift, with which they lend a valuable service to others, the service of the *Yuyaq*, meaning "those who remember." From childhood, they are listened to so that they can grow up to be people whose gestures and words can help the rest of the people return to the center when we become distracted and not able to catch the instructions contained in the light that we breathe. We are humans, forgetful people who do not always produce good decisions easily, and so there are occasions in which help is needed from those born to take care of the attention and memory of us all. I have been witness on multiple occasions to how seemingly chaotic assembly meetings end well. After many divergent points of view have been in conflict, someone has the necessary grace to say something sensible, with great simplicity, uniting hearts and making us feel we have finished a long journey, finally able to stand at the destination we had set out for. In addition, I have noted that the *Yuyaq* that do this have a special capacity in their thinking that makes them naturally able to join rather than separate. They are able to show us, with great calmness, the place where two seemingly irreconcilable truths can come together. And the rest of us accept it easily because, for thousands of years, the culture has shaped us so that we can complement opposites instead of separating them.

THIRD DOOR

❖

A Good Way of
Using Power

13

THE CULTURE OF COMPLEMENTARITY

❖

Our ancestors knew that power used well benefits the world, while power used wrongly destroys the world and harms people. They never used a single power at a time; they always complemented it with another power. The power of will called *Munay*, for example, has as its complementary pair the feminine quality known as *Kuyay*. The will of our heart, our *Munay*, may commit excesses when trying to accomplish its goals at all costs, and so it benefits us to have not only *Munay* but *Kuyay* as well. The Quechua word "*Kuyay*" refers to a feminine quality that helps us act with affection, flexibility, and patience and to cultivate good relationships with others without being imposing, gaining their consent in a warm and respectful way. *Kuyay* and *Munay*, being both talents of the heart, form the healthiest complement. *Munay* gives birth to the actions that create well-being for our loved ones, and

Kuyay provides the tenderness with which we accomplish those actions.

In the southern part of our Andean world, the complement of *Munay* and *Kuyay* have been expressed since remote times through the names of the founders of our culture, who we know as *Manqo Qhapaq* and *Mama Oqllo*. *Manqo Qhapaq*, or "the principal rich and abundant cooking pot," incarnates the principle of *Munay* as the leader that uses its will to contain and "cook" the foods that the sacred sources of life offer us in such a way that they are converted into a source of vitality, instruction, and medicine. And *Mama Oqllo*, or "the mother who incubates," incarnates *Kuyay* as the feminine principle of the care of life, given with warmth, with the affection and unconditional love of a mother. Men can also embody this sacred principle because we each had mothers and other maternal caregivers from whom to learn. These two principles, *Manqo Qhapaq* and *Mama Oqllo*, come together and create the balance that sustains the healthy use of power. One generates the action, and the other generates the necessary care so the action does not cause harm. One prospers in the effort of work, and the other feeds life from the quietude of a tender embrace, like when warmth and food are shared, and enjoying good company becomes more important than goals and accomplishments, which are left outside. And if the first one tries to rush and go out to complete a task, the other kindly asks him not to rush, reminding him that what we work for and what matters most in life are already here with us.

The modern world has forgotten the value of the feminine virtues that rise from *Kuyay*. It considers them weak and a waste of time, so we no longer have as many well-balanced people as there used to be in the old days. Lately, the whole world's culture has been guided by large industrial and commercial ventures. Many successful business leaders, even when they appear to be kind people, have practiced and spread a way of being that separates strategy from heart and intelligence from feeling. They have in essence proposed that if we want to be as wealthy as them, we must try to succeed at all costs, leaving empathy, compassion, and the love of genuine relationships by the wayside. Following their example, we can act in a self-serving way and do harm to others without losing our composure and without causing ourselves any discomfort.

In our ancestral culture, to avoid raising these kinds of leaders who don't offer a good example to others, we established a way of understanding power as being the fruit of a complement of two parts. Every directive, decision, or initiative was always the product of the union of at least two sources, one from above and the other from below, one masculine and one feminine, one human and the other spiritual.

The complementary form of leadership based on the principle of *Yanantin*, "the complement of two that are different," was understood as a generative power. In order to produce good decisions and to give directives, healthy leadership acted in a manner similar to what a man and woman do when, thanks to their being different, they unite to have a child. No one alone can produce something complete and satisfactory. But by complementing their differences, two or more people (and other kinds of life sources) may generate something real, healthy, and lasting. We celebrate the differences that exist among people because dissimilarities complement better than similarities. Regrettably, in the modern world children are invited to play the game of choosing favorites in such a way that, in the presence of two different things, they must choose one and exclude the other. Instead of learning to honor the complementary, they separate things. It has become normal in our times that differences cause a fight—instead of an integration—to see which one prevails over the other. This has impoverished the generative power of humanity in addition to causing wars between countries and the sexes. The wisdom of converting differences into an opportunity to create powerful unions has been lost as well as the ability to pursue conflict to a healthy end until one can see something new emerge from it, something that was much needed and long awaited.

In ancient Cusco and in many areas of the Andean world, communities were divided in two with some living in the upper part and others living in the lower part. And neither group considered themselves superior to the other since they both served the same purpose, generating the balance that sustains the world. Each zone produced something that the other could not. Some important goods that were needed above came from below, and others that were needed below came from above. In the same way, that which restores what belongs on the right comes from the left, and that which restores what belongs to the left comes from the right. And in modern culture, because of the way it values individualism and self-sufficiency, it can be difficult to accept that the masculine has the capacity to restore the feminine and that the feminine has the capacity to restore the masculine. Even harder to accept, what restores order comes from chaos, and what restores chaos comes from order.

14

THE SPIRIT OF
THE GLACIER SPEAKS

❖

I have heard old people from the highlands, as well as the author Juan Carlos Machicado Figueroa, use the word "*Kon*" to name a supernatural power that lives in the ice that shines on the tips of the highest mountains. According to them, *Kon* infuses its sacred power in the mix of ice and light in the glaciers. When the ice melts, this essential source of vitality descends with the water that forms lakes, creeks, and rivers, nourishing everything on its way down to the coast until it joins the sea. In *Muchik*, or *Yunga*—the language of my remote ancestors and a language spoken by people who live closer to the coast—the word "*Kon*" refers to a deity, a sacred bird born from the sea who rises up to the high sky. This sacred bird served our ancestors as an image of the spirit of the sea, rising as vapor and forming clouds that, when reaching the mountains, released the snow and rain that nourished them. In other words, the people in the highlands find the great power of *Kon* in the luminous glacier whose water descends, and the people in the lowlands find it in the luminous sea whose water ascends as it evaporates. And in reality, both are part of the same great power that lives in the circulation of water, illuminated by the Sun, which feeds everything it touches. When it goes up and when it comes down, this sacred power assures the healthy continuation of all life.

Wise people that I have consulted with, like my brother Bacilio, refer to *Kon* in connection with the invisible light (*Illa*) that travels toward the Earth in the darkness of outer space, a light that, in our culture, we consider to be a great source of sacred power and cosmic instructions. The circulation of the great power *Kon* does not begin in the sea or in the glacier; it begins deep in outer space (*Hawaq Pacha*). This must be why my brother Bacilio does not say that *Kon* comes from a glacier because he recognizes the presence of *Kon* before it touches the glacier as a power that lives in the darkness. The light that travels through space arrives on Earth charged with information. During its journey, it gathers information from the stars and then delivers it to the Earth and its inhabitants. Instructions arrive anew each morning, giving us the chance to renew ourselves before dawn each day.

The renewing power of *Kon* can make us feel uplifted,

but it can also provoke our resistance to change. Sometimes it comes to us while we are still sleeping and with so much strength that we may feel uncomfortable without knowing why. Unconsciously, the conservative part of us offers resistance, and then we wake up in a bad mood. Further, when the more conservative part of us feels the touch of the transformative power of the sacred energy of *Kon*, we may perceive the presence of chaos. The comfortable sense of order and the feeling of having things under control can break. This must be why Federico Garcia Hurtado and Pilar Roca Palacio, researchers of the ancient Andean culture, speak in their book *Pachakuteq* of how *Kon* is seen as a source of chaos in some Indigenous communities of the Sacred Valley of Cusco. In my personal experience, apart from encountering the sacred power of *Kon* before first light, I have also encountered it in the chaos of electrical storms, when the sky breaks open and people run to their houses without knowing what will happen or where lightning might strike. Regardless of whether it comes from outer space or from electric storms, *Kon* has the power to renew our lives. In the unpredictable natural context created by a thunderstorm, order remains suspended, replaced by an unstoppable force outside of our control. Thunder roars and lightning strikes in these times of natural disorder. One does not know how long the storm will last, if it's going to rain a lot or a little, or if the rain will leave behind some damage. Even those who predict the weather make mistakes. Rain, water, and life come in this way—by the unpopular means that heaven uses for giving us what we most need.

The great power that generates this momentary loss of order elevates our spirits, shakes us, unblocks us, takes us out of our routine, and leaves us ready to put ourselves in order again but in a better way. Because of this, in our Andean culture we have an immense respect for it. While in modern culture to call something "chaotic" can almost be an insult, ancient wisdom teaches us that chaos and order create healthy complements to one another and that we need to accept both in our lives. We only need to ask ourselves: How often does the transformative power of chaos bring a remedy to what we cannot remedy by ourselves?

Because of its great power, while bringing chaos, sometimes *Kon* can be a very destructive force. It can be as destructive as the cold winds that come from the glacier bringing hail that destroys our crops and all of our work in a matter of minutes. Even this aspect of *Kon*, unwanted due to the suffering it causes, deserves our respect. We have learned to respect the unpredictable, potentially destructive force that, from time to time, returns to bring us to our knees, from a flu that keeps us from work to an earthquake or a severe social conflict. Most people I know would not get mad at these kinds of circumstances and would accept their fates. From my culture, I have learned to respect and even to be grateful to that which has the power to take away my comfort, break my routine, and take from my hands the control of the channels that I normally use to receive information. I am grateful, despite how difficult this can be, because it offers me the chance to be introduced to other channels needed for my development so that I don't remain stuck, wasting the limited time that I have to live this life. If we allow this sacred chaotic and destructive power to do its work and reorder us, it lasts for a short time, and then calm and order return. But when we resist, it tends to stay for a long time.

Our ancestors had so much respect for this great power that they used the word "*Kon*" as part of the composition of a name given to the divine source of life: *Apu Kon Illa Teqsi Wiraqocha Pachayachachiq*, or "Great spirit - source of life - great power of the dark space - foundation of the light - lake of vitality - maker of the knowledge of time-space." And without being afraid of its destructive aspect, they had a relationship with it. Some of our ancestors, the ones most dedicated to developing spiritually, didn't wait to be surprised by the renewing power of *Kon*. Instead, they went searching for it, as many Indigenous people still do. They went out to meet the *Kon* of the dark before sunrise, to feed and renew themselves. And the great power, before bringing them chaos and destruction, gave them instructions. They just had to quiet their minds and breathe with the intention of having their body absorb the cosmic instructions, accepting renewal and even change. Dropping their resistance, they met the great power in the hour when its presence was strongest, choosing wisely to learn from this great instructor before it could become a destructor. They learned by listening instead of waiting to learn by suffering.

Being so close to the sky, the glacier coexists with the *Kon* from outer space and is charged with its power. Seeing this, our ancestors imitated the glacier when intending to be charged by the power of *Kon*. Because of this, in many Andean communities, people wear hats called *Ch'ullo* that in many cases have a white point on the top. And they also imitated the glacier by accepting help from the Sun, the sacred power that complements *Kon* by melting and softening it with its warmth. Even the destructive side of the divine *Kon* can be balanced by the presence of our Father Sun. Thanks to Father Sun, the ice where no life can exist becomes warmer fluid water that runs down to inhabit lakes, streams, rivers, and oceans. Thanks to the Sun and its heat, the sacred energy that can destroy us to recreate us begins to sing in the ravines, calling us to drink and to water our cultivated fields. Thanks to the Sun, we have sufficient warmth and a certain order in the world. We can see with clarity in the daytime, we can count the number of things, and we can count on everything we know to be useful for the sustenance and well-being of our lives. *Urpillay sonqollay taytachayay Inti*—"Thanks, my little Father Sun." Thank you for allowing us to live in this gentle and warm little piece of the powerful Universe. Thank you for the green, for the flowers and the fruits, for the beaches and the meadows along our paths. And thanks, Father Sun, for entering our bodies and growing within us.

When we are nourished by the light, something similar to that which happens in nature also happens within us. Our instructions are the product of the meeting between the sunlight of our being—our awareness, our ability to shine light on something—and that which lives in the radiant black mystery. As we try to increase our awareness and understanding, our internal Sun melts the mystery without killing it, just as the Sun in the sky melts the ice of a glacier, a little each day, just enough for the flow of wisdom from which we can drink to continue living and so that our consciousness does not atrophy.

Wanting to make their understanding and awareness grow, our ancestors had the habit of going near the power of *Kon* each day when it was still dark. But is it correct to speak about this as a place? As if *Kon* were actually a place one can go? In truth, I cannot say that *Kon is* this or that. That it *is* a place, for example. But I can say that *Kon happens*, and to get close to it, we only need to know at what time *Kon* happens.

In our culture, we prefer not to define what the sacred powers *are*, but we appreciate what they *do*. All beings are in motion, changing, and with respect to the forces that guide their ongoing transformation, our Quechua language does not permit the use of the verb "to be" (*Kay*) in third person to define someone or something, treating it like a piece in our puzzle, the puzzle designed by our minds to construct reality. In Quechua, one cannot say that something "is" this or that, as one says in Spanish and in English. One can only say when it arrives, where it is, how it is, with whom it is, or what it is doing. This allows it to avoid being reduced, pigeonholed, or limited. And it is permitted to circulate so that its being can transform and never lose its mystery. As we have seen, with the word "*Kon*" some are referring to a glacier, others to the dark light before dawn, others to the mist of the sea, others to chaos, and others to a sacred destructive force. And we could even use it to name the last Sun of the day, *Kon-ti* in Quechua.

❖

To approach *Kon* and receive its peaceful help, its nondestructive blessing, we can risk being very cold and pray at dawn on the heights of a tall mountain. Or wherever we may find ourselves at the time before the Sun rises, the hour in which it *happens*, we can simply meet its power and breathe in its sacred black light, full of stars. And those who cannot spend the night on a mountain or wake up one or two hours before dawn can look at the water they are about to drink and take a moment to remember that it was, at one time, part of a glacier or in the origin of a storm and that it was so kind to find a way to come to us and give us life. We can greet the water, thank it, and ask for our health because something of that great power lives within it.

Willka Unucha, sacred water, I thank you for giving more life to my life. I ask you to heal me. Repair with your fluidity what you find broken and blocked on the path that the sky uses to come to my Earth, my body. Repair with your light the path that my heart uses to reach the Sun. Let the stars, vibrating in your drops, tell my body the story of universal life and sing the song of total fulfillment. In this hour, although it may be a little late, may I be woken by the same sacred power that woke up the bird of night and made it sing.

15

The Ayar Sisters
and Brothers

❖

Cultures are born and reborn as a result of the reordering that takes place after experiencing severe times of chaos and destruction. At the beginning of a new time, our wise ancestors rebuilt the pillars of our culture, guided by new original instructions. As children, most of us Peruvians had first contact with that original wisdom of the founders of our culture in school. They told us about the pair *Manqo Qhapaq* and *Mother Oqllo*, our great-great-grandparents who emerged together out of the depths of Lake Titiqaqa. We heard the legend of their appearance, which occurred right after the great flood. The two of them had to find a place to found a new civilization and walked to the territory today known as *Qosqo* (Cusco). In school, they told us this story without saying anything about the richness of the principles of life expressed in their names and without recognizing them as the pillars of the wise way of living that our ancestors had that was based on the complementary nature of two opposites. Over time, trespassing over the mental barriers that colonialism built for us, many of us have been able to deepen our understanding, thanks to which we have returned to these legends and made the effort of discovering their secrets, the rich spirituality we carry in our genetic memory, a wisdom we have inherited from our ancestors.

In another version of the origin of our culture, *Manqo Qhapaq* is called *Ayar Manqo*, and his feminine complement is called by the same name, *Mama Oqllo*. In this version, fuller and more aligned with the collective way of life of the Andean people, they are accompanied by three brothers and three sisters, making a total of four couples. We know them as the *Ayar* brothers and sisters who, more than being four men and four women, came to be the expression of eight life principles that guided our ancestral communities.

There are different ways of telling the legend of the *Ayar*. The most common presents them as mythological beings with supernatural powers who appear after the flood with the mission of bringing corn to the place in which they will found a new civilization, the place that today we call Cusco. Grateful to have enjoyed these tales as a child, over time I have come to realize that the four brothers and sisters were eight model spirits. Created by enlightened people in the past, they served to guide people's conduct. To get to know them, one must investigate the meaning of their names. Because Andean culture is based on *Yanantin* (the complement of two that serve each other mutually thanks to their differences) and *Ayni* (the reciprocity that exists between two parts), in order to have the right understanding of the eight principles embodied by the *Ayar*, we need to look at what is born when one of them encounters another.

The complement of the first two, *Ayar Manqo* and *Mama Oqllo* (the principal container of light, and the mother who incubates), has to do with the union of the sacred masculine and the sacred feminine that, in addition to helping us avoid the abuse of power that I mentioned before, also guarantees the reproduction and continuity of life. The balance that sustains entire communities and their environments comes from a masculine source who firmly offers direction and provides a solid container for life and its dynamics. And it comes from a feminine source as well, who provides the warmth of affection and the profound loving wisdom that supports the healthy growth of everything and everyone. Always walking with "her" on our left and "him" on our right, we have the ability to accomplish our goals without causing harm to others.

Next comes the second complement, *Ayar Kachi* and *Mama Wak'o*. *Ayar Kachi*, the guardian of salt (in charge of the economy) and *Mama Wak'o*, the guardian of the sacred, manifest a balance absent in the modern world, in which economists easily forget the value of the sacred, and those of us who live enamored of the sacred can be very bad economists. Money did not exist in the ancient Andean-Amazonian world, nor was there large land ownership. Land belonged to those who worked it, and the surplus production was taken to the communitarian *Qolqas*, storage units full of different products available for those who most needed them. Among these products was salt (*Kachi*) and meat preserved with salt. There were *Qolqas* in all the territories of the ancient Andean-Amazonian world from which many products were redistributed in the different climate zones so that neither drought nor plague would cause any community to be left without food and so that the abundance produced in the good years might compensate for lack during the less good years. And just as there existed thousands of *Qolqas*, there were also thousands of *Wak'as* near them. The *Wak'as* were places in which sacred objects were cared for—objects used as instruments to communicate with the heart of the Earth, the heart of the Universe, the *Apus*, and the original sources of the products guarded in the *Qolqas*. All the powerful spirits that helped create abundance were cared for in the *Wak'as* and also in the lakes, forests, mountains, rivers, springs, and oceans, all places considered to be depositories of the sacred. Professionals, such as economists and administrators, were considered just as important as those who were spiritual servants (who in some places were also referred to as *Wak'a* or *Wak'o*) since people knew that caring for the sacred sources maintains the balance and health of the world, just as a good economic system does. *Mama Wak'o* reminds *Ayar Kachi* that he is welcome to use the Earth to produce and distribute in an efficient manner but that he must not do it in a way that damages the sacred sources of life.

In some of the stories about the *Ayar* brothers and sisters, *Mama Wak'o* appears as a very powerful warrior, able to protect the sacred with determination, balancing *Ayar Kachi*, who appears as a powerful man, able to move mountains and alter the currents of rivers. According to one ancient legend, once after *Ayar Kachi* had used excessive force to change something in nature, he was overthrown by his sister, *Mama Wak'o*, and then made prisoner in a mountain by the other siblings to stop him from causing any more damage. Applying this story to the reality of the modern world ruled by human supremacy, we could say that the industrious *Ayar Kachi* is on the loose making tremendous alterations to nature for the sake of increasing production and that there is no wisdom at the moment able to complement or guard the sacred by arresting him. The efforts of different organizations trying to arrest the destruction of various forms of life that exist on Earth remind me of how the other *Ayar* siblings tried to block the actions of *Ayar Kachi*. And *Mama Wak'o* reminds me of the groups of Indigenous people from all over the world who, for decades, have tried to have their voices be heard, telling us that if we don't take care of the sacred and respect the sources of life, we may end up destroying our world. There is a radical difference now illustrated by the fact that while the powerful *Mama Wak'o* had the ability of stopping her brother in ancient times, in our times many Indigenous activists who protect life in their own lands end up being assassinated. How incredible that, thousands of years in the past, before industries existed, and when there were not so many people, wise ones proposed creating a culture capable of taking advantage of the gifts of the economist, *Ayar Kachi*, as long as it was complemented by the feminine wisdom that guards the sacred.

The third complement was embodied by *Mama Ipakura* (older aunt/chief aunt) and *Ayar Auqa* (the warrior). The older aunt who has authority and the warrior that guards the fire respond to the necessity to maintain social order and the health of the community through discipline. The value expressed through them contains the necessary wisdom of differentiating children from adults so they can be treated differently as they are formed or corrected.

So that children do not doubt the unconditional love of

their parents, *Mama Ipakura* has the responsibility of doing the unpopular and little-appreciated work of correcting them. She trains children and youngsters using her feminine wisdom without domesticating them. She helps them develop the necessary boundaries so they will not get hurt and not cause harm to others nor to their sacred world. The older aunt combines her firm authority and her affectionate feminine side to call attention to those who are distracted and offers them healing because she also knows how to talk to healing plants. She uses medicinal plants and discipline to stop the imbalances that harm people before they go too far and thereby helps young ones grow up healthy. Many of the medicines she uses are bitter, but she is prepared to make the sacrifice of not always being loved or appreciated.

On the other side of *Mama Ipakura* stands the warrior *Ayar Auqa*, who has the power to care for the sacred fire without letting it go out, even when it rains or hails. As a warrior, he can also use his force to demand discipline and give punishments to adults who put the health of the community in danger, whether they come from the community itself or from other places. This masculine quality of the warrior, who can even spill blood to protect his people, can be too strong for children. Until a certain age, it is better for them to grow in a feminine space and learn from someone who has the intuition for choosing the right medicine when it is time to correct others. *Mama Ipakura* and *Ayar Auqa* complement one another so that the force of the warriors does not harm the tenderness of the community.

Finally, we have the complement of *Mama Rewe* (Ovum) and *Ayar Uchu* (Chili). The guardian of feminine changes and the guardian of spice create a complement that lets people live relaxed and with joy. *Ayar Uchu* provides, to people used to working hard in challenging natural environments, potent spices that give delicious flavor to life (the same spices Christopher Columbus was seeking). He reminds us that playing and having joyful moments balances us. Without them we can accumulate bitterness and cannot live well nor be wise at work. The spice of life gives us better character when fulfilling our obligations, using our authority, loving someone, offering guidance, and trying to resolve big problems. The guardian of spice also prepares the rituals for encountering the sacred and organizes festivities so that people will enjoy themselves and nourish themselves from the natural power that exists on special dates. In this case *Ayar Uchu*, conscious of the cycles of nature and of the cosmos that influence the state of life on Earth, invites us to celebrate ceremonial festivals that help us be in sync with the actual cosmic times in which we live. In this way, he helps us do all our activities according to a natural calendar, living in harmony with the rhythm of nature. During ceremonies and community celebrations, *Ayar*

Uchu invites people to not take the tribulations of material life and the dramas of the human condition too seriously and encourages us to enjoy spiritual fullness in moments of pure well-being. The spicy fire of *Ayar Uchu*, different from the fire of the warrior *Ayar Auqa*, serves to bring happiness and joy, to channel sexual and sensual energy in ways that make our life more beautiful. The enjoyment of life through those rituals, which are made on important cosmic dates like the beginning of spring or the day of the big harvest, helps us openly welcome, with much gratitude and respect, the power that rises above us—the immense power of nature.

Everything said with respect to *Ayar Uchu* applies as well to *Mama Rewe* except that she, being feminine, carries wonderful mysteries. She embodies, in a natural and fluid way, the principles that *Ayar Uchu* inculcates in the rest. *Rewe* means "ovum." *Mama Rewe*, who lives under the influences of the lunar cycles, has the wisdom to remind us that everything changes. To be able to adapt ourselves and not suffer when things change, we must cultivate the flexibility of a dancer and the acceptance of a truly humble person. *Mama Rewe* makes us honor the sacred time of women's menstruation that, under the influence of the moon, creates changes in their waters, their fertility, their feelings, and their understandings. She teaches us to not take our plans too seriously and to not be rigid in our course of action since everything can change. With her, we learn to be humble in front of the great power of the Universal Mother and to receive the surprises life brings with acceptance, even when they were not what we had planned. She reminds us that the sacred source of wisdom can veil itself in darkness and that we can hear her without seeing her. Powerful natural movements that we cannot control are constantly influencing our lives, and both *Mama Rewe* and *Ayar Uchu* remind us that we do better respecting them and adapting to them than trying to control them.

❖

Many people in our country wonder if the *Ayar* brothers and sisters really existed as flesh-and-blood people or if we should just consider them to be mythological beings. In my humble opinion, neither of these possibilities excludes the other. As I said earlier, first they were spirits (today called mythological beings) created by a wise, ancient culture. And then we had actual people in different moments of our history whose lives were a manifestation of the principles contained in their names. As our good brother Manari has said, that which we sow in the spirit world appears in the material world. By consistently calling upon the *Ayar* and the principles expressed by their names, our ancestors consecrated their existence in the spirit world, which was then reflected in the material world, first through the skill of some great female and male leaders (to whom the names of the *Ayar* were given) and then through the patterns of behavior of people in thousands of Andean communities.

16

LEAD WITH INTEGRITY

❖

Nutritionists teach us that a balanced diet should contain protein, fiber, fat, and carbohydrates. When our body receives these four nutrients in a balanced way, our chances for good health increase. Without disrespecting what nutritionists recommend, I want to call attention to the fact that the names chosen by our ancestors for the four male *Ayar* brothers also refer to food: a Sacred Pot (*Manqo*), salt (*Kachi*), fire (*Auqa*), and chili (*Uchu*). Going deeper, remembering that these names also relate to life principles, we can recognize that, for our ancestors, health did not depend only on a good balance of protein, fiber, fat, and carbohydrates. It depended also on the internalization and integration of profound human qualities. The complement that each one of the *Ayar* brothers creates with one of their four sisters—*Mama Oqllo*, *Mama Wak'o*, *Mama Ipakura*, and *Mama Rewe*—gives us important clues related to the wholeness of our being.

From the point of view of our ancient culture, we understand that our satiety and our health depend on cultivating eight qualities in our interiors. These eight qualities are guided by eight spirits, the first being *Manqo*, the Sacred Pot, the solid body that contains the other seven. Their enormous relevance to our health and integrity as *Runa* beings can be found, even more profoundly than in their number, in their unity, in the fact that they remain well-integrated thanks to the power of the Sacred Pot that contains them. And so, I ask, could they still complement each other to create the balance in each one of us if they separate or if one of them goes off on their own? And what would happen if the Sacred Pot were broken? Seeing these eight qualities as parts of our interior, as the content of our being, we can understand that our integrity comes from their union, complementary nature, and good relationship. The principle of *Manqo Qhapaq*, presented by our ancestors as the foundation of our culture, is carried by each of us in our bodies to assure the integration of everything that we have inside us, to keep the balance of our wise, natural order. When we are integrated, the Universe can grow, illuminate, and flourish within us just as it does in every other cosmic and terrestrial body. Without integration, without a cohesive power in our interior, we cannot hold our inner parts together, and eventually "our teeth fall out"—we lose the ability to nourish ourselves with more content from the sources of life.

The unnatural system of life that predominates nowadays, guided by human supremacy, requires a lack of integrity in order to function as it does. Imposed on the majority of humans, this normalized lack of integrity neglects not only the nature of the outdoors but also the nature that lives within each person, creating a society full of sick people. Any manifestation of human supremacy, in itself, destroys integrity. Those who believe that a human being can rise above their own earthly nature will have much difficulty when it comes to integrating the natural life that feeds and now lives inside of them. Nature from which we extract materials, nature that feeds us, and nature that lives within us are all the same. Neglecting or disrespecting any of these versions of nature disrespects them all, inflicting self-harm. On the other hand, those who have taken good care of the natural sources of their food and have welcomed and integrated inside their "sacred pots" the air they breathe, the light they breath, the land that feeds them, and the beings who have given their lives to feed them become satiated and grateful and do not cause harm. They become part of everything that has fed them and, knowing themselves to be nature, cannot easily betray nor feel superior to her. Perhaps they can cause destruction without malice, just as excessive rain naturally creates a flood, but to prevent too much of this, our ancestors gave us life principles, spirits that guide us so that we do not become a devastating force, so that we remain aware and occupy a role in nature as guardians of balance.

Lack of integrity has become a large problem, and as of now we are out of balance and thus incapable of guarding the balance of nature. Many have become used to being lazy, to being indolent, to living without the force of *Munay*, and so it seems normal to not make an effort to care for nature when making decisions about what to produce or consume or how to dispose of the waste it creates. Similarly, for many, it has become normal to promise something and then to fail to keep one's word. In the current moment, our Indigenous communities are going along with this tendency that is so present in modern life, and our people are in danger of acquiring a new habit of accepting corruption as something normal. Often, we hear it said of elected authorities, "It's OK to rob as long as they do their work." But in reality, of course it is not right that they rob us while they work for us. Nor is it benign that they lie to us. In the end, the use of power to benefit only a few prevents its ability to benefit us all.

How good it would be if, in the present day, we had the same customs and values that the ancient Andean-Amazonian people had in antiquity. They were so strong and had so much *Munay* that they were able to keep their word. The concentrated energetic content within their "sacred pots" gave them the power needed to act with integrity, without betraying themselves or their fellow humans or their Mother Earth. Sadly, since the time of colonization when our "sacred pots" were broken, we have begun to acquire other habits. Some of the people of old communities believed that, in order to survive, they had to follow the example of the conquistadors, who knew how to win wars by lying and how to bring more food into their homes by stealing. Even as fervent Christians, the conquistadors had great weaknesses that caused them to betray their own religious principles. This left a terrible example that some of our Andean people follow to this day.

Today, the systems of modern societies depend upon a lack of integrity in order to stay alive. If there were integrity—above all among leaders who make the most important decisions and who have promised to help people—the system of living based on deceit and the exploitation of people, leaving workers unsatisfied, destroying the Earth, polluting water and air, and harming trees and animals could not continue to exist. Destructive ambition and lack of integrity have been forming a solid partnership. Corruption exists not only when someone does an act that is against the law but also in any situation where someone causes harm to nature or to people even when they are not technically breaking legal norms. Institutionalized corruption protects companies and the stable social order that contributes to the success of such companies while destroying the stability of natural resources that many companies use to create their products. In this way, humanity has devolved into a very primitive state. In the cases of some political or business leaders, their lack of empathy for those who are harmed seems to be the product of a lack of integrity that they have within themselves. Their hearts seem not to be integrated with their spirits, their bodies seem not to be integrated with their minds, and they seem unable to hear all that speaks within them. Carried only by greed, competition, "reason," or their addiction to luxury and comfort, these brothers and sisters of ours ignore other voices that ask them, from within, to stop before they cause harm to a community, a woman, a child, a man, an animal, plants, the water, the air, or even themselves.

For thousands of years we thought that the glaciers who we consider our *Apus* would always be there, like the sky, and could never disappear. But now, due to global warming, we see for the first time the imminent disaster. Brothers and sisters from the lower parts of the world have lost their integrity, and over time, the effect of their neglect has come to our high Andean territories. We wish to humbly share our memory with them so they may remember their own ancient wisdom. With all respect, we want them to hear what we have to say. Otherwise, we will be the ones who will continue to learn new customs, originated in other societies, that will bring us to achieve great "successes" at the cost of losing our happiness, our hearts, our glaciers, and the jungle. Beyond simply wanting to preserve our beautiful culture, we are facing an emergency situation, a series of threats to our continued existence. The generalized corruption of leaders and people of influence in the modern world has been placed in front of us like a barrier. It is the largest impediment to the solution for the problems that threaten not only the continuity of human life but also all the other beings in nature that live with us. Corruption and the excessive ambition that accompanies it prevents leaders from agreeing upon the urgent changes we must make to stop the destruction of our natural home. Some of the people who possess the most material wealth do not want to lose what they have even though the world is being destroyed around them. New entrepreneurs seek opportunities to improve their chances of creating a personal fortune, as if it were their turn and as if it were their birthright, without thinking of the consequences. There are also discussions on the world stage about what needs to change, but these conversations are far from sufficient and do not have the power to create the necessary actions. In the meantime, our lives are in danger. The house is burning, and the fire chiefs are sitting around comfortably, discussing how it would be convenient to put out the fire and when. More than immoral, this seems to be the consequence of an incapacity, a clear lack of *Munay*, a serious deficit of attention, or a terrible lack of love for life.

Lack of integrity does not begin with a moral question, but instead it begins with an incapacity. For it to exist, there must first have been a disconnection between those inner parts that allow us to be the wonderful, gifted beings that, in truth, we are. The head gets disconnected from the heart, the mind from the body, sexuality from the heart, masculine from the feminine, power from love, and the material from the spiritual. In accord with the principles of our inherited culture, from the time of the *Yachaywasi* (the houses of ancestral wisdom) we understand that, in order to have integrity, a *Runa* must become integrated, a never-ending task that requires that we increase our energy and know how to contain it well. It also requires that we have a strong commander in the center, a strong heart, otherwise one can become indecisive and be easily corrupted. To promote the integrity of leaders and of everyone else, our ancestors didn't use religious or moral rules, nor the kind of authority that manipulates people through fear of punishment. They used life practices and rituals that helped individuals increase their personal sacred power and become integrated within themselves. These practices and rituals were born from their knowledge of human nature, from knowing that the efforts we make in order to become integrated are constantly interrupted by forgetfulness. Therefore, they built community meeting spaces where they could return to look at themselves, look at each other, communicate with each other, and heal themselves, through awareness, from the personal disasters caused by oblivion. And then, without enforcement, only when their own will determined, individuals could choose to renew their commitments to keep learning and to keep increasing the content of light inside their "sacred pots."

17

Bring Our Energy Back to the Center

❖

We have more stored and concentrated energy to sustain our efforts when we unify our internal parts. We cannot function as a solid container of light before having reached a certain level of unification, aligning our internal parts. Without sufficient personal power, preventing our internal contents from being dispersed and constantly lost becomes a difficult task. For the most part, our internal contents behave as if they were a stack of cut wheat, loosely blowing at the mercy of the wind. Each stalk, each part of our dispersed being, has experiences as ephemeral as a brief flash of light. We feel something deeply, our thoughts are suddenly illuminated, we see something, we have a moment of wisdom, we make some good decisions, and soon we forget it all, losing it. But to our benefit, this tendency starts to change after we become consolidated. Once we become solid, like a good clay cooking pot, we can contain, unite, and slowly "cook" our experiences, the opportunities that life offers us. And instead of ending up dispersed or lost, our life experiences, chosen or destined, become nourishment for our character and growth.

When we look at ourselves, we can discover elements of our interior world that operate on their own, separate from the rest, fragile and unrooted, susceptible to external influences that cause them to easily get lost. This explains why it happens so frequently that we become aware of something important moving within us, we feel something and begin to look at it, but soon we forget it, without having identified its origin, losing the opportunity to go more deeply into self-knowledge. And until we have begun to unify our internal parts, owning all that lives within ourselves, our will remains weak and unstable, and our personality constantly changes. The different parts that live inside take turns getting what they need (or want) in a given moment. And while each of them has a proper function to fulfill, we have a problem every time they compete to govern the body or when one of them wins and ends up dominating, taking charge for a while at the expense of other parts, which stop developing and expressing themselves. At certain moments, the rational mind takes the lead, and one loses the capacity to feel. At other times, sexual desire governs the mind completely, and one can no longer think. The eyes get clouded by an avalanche of emotions, and one can no longer see with clarity the person who is right in front of them nor hear what they really want to tell us. In this way, our different internal parts take turns presenting themselves as our "I," when in reality none of them alone has everything it takes to be our complete selves.

It becomes difficult for the power of *Munay* to grow in the center of a person whose energy remains dispersed and scattered. And without *Munay* such individuals often end up doing what they do not want to do and not doing what they really want to do. As long as the true desire in the center of someone's being continues to be weak, the only thing that will count is what they want today, which another part of them will not want tomorrow. There is a need to increase the power of one's presence, the light that shines within a *Runa's* center, a power much like a Sun creating orbits for its planets or like an eagle that can see all of one's parts from above, guiding them, helping bring the whole of oneself into accord. We have many minds that need to be in accord. We may observe the mind of air, a fabric woven from threads of energy, governing our intellect. Similarly, we may observe the mind of water (emotions), the mind of fire (sexuality) and the mind of earth (bodily functions). Several minds live in our interiors, each with its desires, its fears, and its own voice, aspiring to govern and satisfy its singular needs. And in the middle of this disorder, the heart awakens, trying to acquire the necessary presence to become the center of gravity that calls all the parts into a unity.

We should not ignore the need to grow our sacred personal power and become the masters of ourselves. If we do not succeed in bringing all of our inner parts into alignment, all that we do in order to accomplish our aims will only bring dissatisfaction. Something in us wishes to come fully into being, and if it does not grow enough, we become sad. Something in us wishes to bear fruit, much like a tree. The feeling of absence may be very difficult to bear when we find we do not have something to give. But the opposite can happen too, over time, when thanks to the efforts we make, our internal contents begin to mature and we become givers of light. When our little internal Sun grows, we become the fruitful beings we truly wish to be.

❖

Before colonization, everything I have shared here and much more was remembered and in some way practiced in sacred places called *Yachaywasi*. *Yachay* means "wisdom" and *Wasi* means "house." The *Yachaywasi* were small *Wak'as* located inside large *Wak'as*, today called temples or archaeological centers, where some of the young people went to receive instructions from wise elders, their mentors, some of whom were flesh-and-blood humans.

In the *Yachaywasi* they had a practice called *Walthay* that consisted of causing energy to come back to our centers, creating a cohesion among our internal parts. The practice of *Walthay* was accompanied by the ancient custom of binding the internal contents through the use of *Watanas*, (*Watanakuna* in Quechua), or ties. Since anyone can suffer from leaks of vital energy—mental, emotional, and sexual— the apprentices of *Yachaywasi* used ties to bind their inner contents and not lose them, a custom still practiced in our Andean-Amazonian culture today. In many communities, we still understand that everything that has a material function also has an energetic or vibrational function. Clothes, jewelry, and different pieces of traditional ornaments that we use to adorn our bodies not only protect and beautify us but also help to bind our energy. As part of a daily discipline, apprentices of the ancient *Yachaywasi* wisdom schools used *Watanas* (something that serves as a tie), which they wove to place on different parts of the body with the intention of binding their content of light. Headbands, or ties for the forehead, are called *Llawtu*. Those that swaddle the waist are called *Chumpi*. Bracelets for the wrist are called *Ch'ipana*. And anklets for the feet are called *Chaki Watana*. For women, it was, and continues to be, important to use the *Chumpi* on their waistlines to contain the energy of the womb, the sacred place of both water and the moon, where they store their feminine energy in complement to the solar energy that they store (just as men do) in the lower part of their chests.

For the youth in the ancient world, the use of *Watanas* must have been something very natural since they were simply doing for themselves what their parents did for them just after they were born—swaddling them from their feet to their neck and putting a *Ch'ullo* (cap) on their heads—a custom that some Andean communities still practice today having observed that babies who are swaddled become young people with greater physical strength and with a greater will than those who are not swaddled. Today when the wise women of our community remind another woman that she needs to swaddle her waist or to swaddle her baby, they say "*Walthay*," which means "tie the energy to make it return to the center."

Speaking about the wisdom of the teachers of the *Yachaywasi* does not place the wisdom of the people in the communities in an inferior position. In the original Andean-Amazonian culture, there was no strong separation between "those who know" and "those who don't" because everyone had access to knowledge transmitted orally. In antiquity, the teachers and apprentices of the *Yachaywasi*, the wise elders in the farming communities, and the members of the families were all integrated, united by the same cultural thread, by the same winds, by the free distribution of knowledge. We may assume that it was the wise teachers of the *Yachaywasi* who instructed the people in the communities, but there also exists the possibility that, in some cases, it happened the other way around. Could it be that there were farmers, mid-wives, and hunters who taught the teachers of the *Yachaywasi* practices such as *Walthay* (bringing the energy of the body to center)? In accordance with the way our culture functions, where things move from above to below, and from below to above, it could have happened either way. The people of the *Yachaywasi*, when they visited the villages, were like the glacier water that flows down, and when the people from the villages visited the *Yachaywasi*, they were like the sea that rises as mist. And this circulation of energy generated a culture full of sacred power in which everyone complemented one another and learned from everyone else.

Curiously, not knowing this, the conquistadors were committed to enforcing the closing of the *Yachaywasi* so that the ancient wisdom would not continue to be imparted. But they did not count on the fact that it could also be found in the communities and within the homes of the common people. Thanks to this, and in spite of the fact that the *Yachaywasi* fell into disuse for centuries, we still know something of what was practiced in them because people in Quechua- and Aimara-speaking communities still have customs in which the memory of the ancient knowledge was preserved. Among these customs that still live we find *Walthay*—practiced in a natural, spontaneous way without a need for any formal training. The action of centering the energies of the body produces a state of being that has become important for us to cultivate, and in the use of *Watanas* to bind the internal contents we find a physical way of helping ourselves accomplish this aim. At a deeper level, those of us who have inherited knowledge related to the *Watanas* we adorn ourselves with believe that, for experienced adults, the need of tying our inner contents only requires humble self-observation. The most experienced *Runa* only need to feel the moment in which they are losing or misusing their energy to immediately bring it back to their center (*chaupi*), simply through awareness, back to the place where their internal Sun wants to grow.

GIVE SHAPE TO OUR SPIRIT

❖

In antiquity, just as today, a young person could meet their mentors in any place they visited or in the same place they lived. There were always wise grandparents in the family and in the community. But in antiquity, very probably, a greater opportunity for learning was found in the *Yachaywasi*, where leaders and great teachers were formed throughout thousands of years. Sadly, during the times of the conquest, especially due to that violent practice that the Christians called "the extirpation of the idols," there was a very severe interruption of our culture through the systematic destruction of sacred spaces and objects. Since then, generations of talented young people have been denied the possibility of attending a *Yachay-wasi* to receive their inheritance of ancient instructions. New leaders, European military authorities, and Catholic priests stuck their swords through the *Wak'as*.

The interruption of our sacred culture occurred in the

Wak'as, but resistance to a complete interruption occurred in the homes of common people and their communities, especially when they were far from large population centers created during colonization. But despite their determined, peaceful resistance, the sacred culture, which before was an infinite river that came down from the sky and circulated along the earth before returning skyward, was converted into a thin trickle with just enough force to prevent it from becoming totally stagnant. The annual festivals, the rituals, the work of the keepers of tradition, and the powerful contents of our original languages maintained this small stream and kept it alive. And the stream continued on its way toward us, the heirs of the ancient culture living in this time. We are grateful for the teachings that have come down to us from the past, teachings that help us know how to form our spirits. And still, we yearn for the profundity of the river that existed before, for the possibility of submerging ourselves in it completely. We want to live enjoying an intimate relationship with the sacred in everyday life with the magic of the *Wak'as* always within reach. We would like to feel the presence of the sacred world in the streets, when we shop, when we dress, in all the work that we do, and above all when we see our children walking to school to receive their education.

The interruption of our culture occurred in the *Yachaywasi* that existed within the great *Wak'as*, such as *Machu Picchu*,

Saksaywaman, *Intiwatana,* and hundreds more, sacred places that we go to when we want to visit our ancestral memory. Among the beautiful memories kept in the great *Wak'as* also lives a wound, the damage done to us by blocking the possibility of our continuing to develop our spirits as our ancestors did. Given the brutality and severity of those acts, most of the world thought that the wound was mortal, and indeed it seemed to be. But when centuries pass and the wounded don't die, we begin to see them as immortal. And sooner or later, if death does not take them, life does. And once fully recovered, they inevitably become stronger than before—this has always been the case. We are recovering, little by little. We don't know how many people there are today in our Andean-Amazonian territory trying to increase their content of light in order to form their spirits as was done in the past, but certainly we are many, and we may be slow, but we are doing it. Thankfully, times have changed and colonialism has lost some of its imposing force. Nowadays, no one needs to feel ashamed for trying to develop spiritually as the ancients did, wearing *Watanas* to bind the energy content of their body, making offerings to request help from the *Apus*, and visiting ancient *Wak'as* to listen to them and to recover memory.

Speaking for myself and for the sisters and brothers with whom I share a spiritual path, I can affirm that those who do this work know that, due to the enormous amount of distractions offered by the modern world, we are taking a long time to form our "sacred pots" and to become solid containers of light. Unless we had the mentoring of grandparents that loved the old ways, we had to begin from zero when we were no longer children, accepting the call that urged us to make the first effort. Now, without doubt, we are growing spiritually. And we can never forget that the first attempts we made, like any apprentice, led us to observe ourselves and to know ourselves from the inside. The first agreements we were able to provoke among all our internal parts were made with a will that was still very weak, needing help, and receiving help. We had to have humility to listen to another will much more powerful than our own that was guiding us from the heart of the Universe. Its call produced a feeling in us, a profound yearning and irresistible desire to wake up. And since then, this call returns over and over again in different forms and continues saving us from the death-in-life that comes from forgetting oneself.

In order to form our spirits, in addition to remembering and feeding the spirits that guide us, we are dedicated to knowing and identifying our internal parts and persevering in the attempt to bring them all under a single agreement. In sacred moments of power, we hold and tie, in an elegant and harmonious way, the different strings of energy we find loose and scattered inside of our four minds, the minds of air, water, fire, and earth. Through years of experience, both succeeding and failing in our attempts to unify ourselves, we see our capacities grow, little by little. On occasion, we get to have enough focused energy so as to be able to give all our attention to the sacred power that arrives bringing a gift. And as time passes, thanks to these gifts, our content of light grows. We also become more integrated and more accustomed to not abandoning ourselves, living closer to the sacred fire that shines in the center of our being. Now there can be magical nights where we have the ability to tie our mind to the mind of the Earth, to the mind of the Sun, and to the mind of everything we want to know, be it a plant, a mountain, a jaguar, a lake, or a constellation of stars. We experience *Yuyay* (the state of being in which thinking, remembering, and understanding become the same) as our ancestors did when making their own investigations, the ones that brought them to make the great discoveries they applied to their agricultural work, their way of reading the stars, their systems of irrigation, their architecture, their ceremonial art, and their sophisticated, respectful ways of organizing both as a community and as a nation. For them, the knowledge acquired thanks to their *Hamautakuna* (teachers) was important, but even more important was to cultivate those states of awareness in which the heart and the mind are aligned with the spirit of a sacred source. To do that, they dedicated time to silence, to contemplation, to concentrating their minds, to patient observation, to opening their hearts, and to the affectionate art of communication with the *Apus*, praying and imploring to be "worked," with the *Apu* acting as sculptor and themselves as the clay. Within the means of our own potential, we try to follow the example of our ancestors.

In our collective culture, we promote good relationships and not individualism, understanding that the elevation of our spirits, while requiring individual effort, doesn't happen as a personal achievement. As individuals, we require a lot of help, as well as humility for receiving that help, like turning ourselves into clay and letting another shape us in the same way towering mountains allow wind and water to shape them. Even the people who are closest to us teach us things we did not know and often make us see things about ourselves that we were totally unaware of. We are also ready to meet wise mentors. In our culture, mentors act with such humility that, for the most part, they simply help us encounter the spirits that can guide us, spirits whose influence produces a certain character in us, a way of singing that we use to call for what we most need.

❖

Things have changed since our countries have become multicultural, and I want to respect the fact that today there are many people in the Andean-Amazonian communities who are forming their spirits in alliance with spirits brought by the Spanish. Since the conquest, syncretism has been produced by joining the spirits of our *Apus* and Catholic spirits. In their relationships with saints and virgins, the people have been able to continue encountering the old deities that their ancestors fed. And this happened because, in order to survive the interruption of our culture caused by the extirpation of idolatries, and in order to not die of hunger, some important *Apus* allied themselves with spirits fed by the Catholic faith who received them and hid them behind their images. These *Apus*, hidden behind a Christ, a virgin, or a saint, were able to continue helping people in a camouflaged way. Receiving food in the Catholic festivals that were permitted, many ancient deities have been able to continue helping for centuries, in secret, to stop wars and to reduce natural disasters, protecting and healing people without judging their new beliefs. For their part, the people felt grateful for having survived and continued feeding those holy spirits with devotion no matter what clothes they wore. Actually, before taking them out in a procession, they dress them themselves, making them shine with silver and gold, colorful as our mountain flowers in the harvest month. And how good that those who need to pray have someone that marvelous to pray to! The love with which our people pray causes their spirits to be elevated and to shine. In the end, I believe that a profound and grateful affection, born in our insides, not motivated by fear or desire, shapes our spirit more than anything. It erases the worst doubts and allows us to continue walking in life with enough confidence to carry on.

Collective Enlightenment

❖

Something very precious that has not changed since ancient times, even though we are now multicultural, is rooted in the value we give to collective life. We continue seeing ourselves as members of a group, for which we feel a lot of affection. If there were a hero, it would be the group and not an individual. Because in truth, no one can accomplish something important by themselves. Also, making the effort to learn, to grow, to form our luminous spirits, only makes sense when it becomes a shared happiness. Human happiness comes from not feeling alone, from feeling that one belongs to something, from feeling that one belongs to the heart of someone. Happiness grows when we share it with others. Therefore, the apprentices of the *Yachaywasi* of ancient times, whose footsteps we try to follow, never stopped being members of a community nor withdrew permanently from their loved ones. When they immersed themselves in the dark side of a house of wisdom, in a cave, or in the depths of the jungle, they only stayed there for a period of time. Then they returned to their people to continue their work and to develop their discipline while still being part of a couple and of a family, surrounded by their children and their community full of brothers and sisters. In the same way, those of us who practice tying our energy in order to augment our content of light and to shape our spirits do not need to distance ourselves from the collective world in which we live. We don't need to stay away from our loved ones in order to protect ourselves from the temptations and distractions of human life that could make us lose our energy. On the contrary, being exposed to possible distractions helps us practice *Walthay*, the art of returning to our center over and over again.

In the Andean-Amazonian culture, personal enlightenment doesn't have to be the ultimate aim in the life of an apprentice. To become enlightened without including others has no sense in a communitarian world. And even if some of our people would arrive at a state of enlightenment and experience the crystalization of their internal Sun, the aim of the entire effort would include being able to generate abundance for the community, abundance of water and food and of the collective spiritual joy that is produced when, together, we feel and celebrate the unity of everything and everyone.

The ancients, whose wisdom we attempt to follow, learned to cultivate their skills to generate a type of abundance that was material and spiritual at the same time, drawing energy down from the powerful vitality of the Universe, to make it circulate through their hands for their work and through their hearts to share the fruits of their labor. Works made on the material plane, such as the production of food, the construction of infrastructure, the making of textiles, and cooking, were always elevated to a sacred level with the help of the known collective rituals, which added to the beautiful spontaneous gestures born from the hearts of the people.

Due to the culture giving priority to collective achievements, the Andean-Amazonian world was always rich, except when it suffered severe natural disasters. From what we know about the times before the annihilation of the idols carried out by the colonizers, I can affirm that it was a world where neither material nor spiritual hunger existed. The people of the communities (*Ayllu*), after refining both their human and their spiritual aspects, created abundance through constant and respectful communication with the natural sources of life with whom they had a love story. The fields were watered with the joy from the hearts of grateful people whose everyday life, difficult but full of cultural riches, was able to include the material and the spiritual simultaneously. Even inevitable human failings were greeted with simplicity, humor, and compassion as part of the beauty of the world. I know it was like this because it continues to be so today.

20

To Tie the Sun

❖

The wise ones versed in ancient traditions provided the apprentices in the *Yachaywasi* opportunities to receive instructions, mediated by spiritual experiences, in places of work made sacred by the high vibrational frequencies of their stone altars known as *Intiwatana* (something that serves to tie the Sun). Some of those who learned to use *Watanas* to tie the light contained in their bodies also learned to use the *Intiwatana* to tie the energy that came from the Sun to their territory, creating a field of sacred power that permeated the entire terrestrial space where they lived.

Due to the number of incorrect interpretations that have circulated for centuries, I want to clarify that these *Inti-watana* altars—in addition to serving as ways of measuring the movements of the earth, the stars, and the passage of time like a clock—acted as instruments to anchor the energies and instructions emanating from cosmic events for the beneficial use of the *Runa*. The changes in time were acknowledged with the help of *Intiwatana* altars and other *Wankas* (standing stones) by spiritual workers and astronomers who observed the arrival of the solstices and equinoxes, the new cosmic year, lunar cycles, certain constellations arriving at the center of the sky, and other cosmic events whose powerful energies strongly influence the occurrences of life on Earth. And just as that which farms produce can remain dissipated and abandoned until it degrades on the vine, so too that which the Universe produces and offers to us may remain scattered and wasted. Therefore, in the same way that we gathered and stored products until it is time to put them into the cooking pot, the *Wak'as* with *Intiwatana* altars functioned first and foremost as receptors that harvested cosmic information and then as depositories, large containers like "cooking pots" carefully designed to "cook" and to make digestible the sacred cosmic energies that arrived charged with instructions and opportunity.

Those who worked in the great *Wak'as* knew how to harvest sacred power and how to cook energies using rays of light and stars reflected in water. They greeted these "ingredients" with the power of the human heart through sacred speech, music, singing, and dancing. In rituals, they blew lines of energy toward the sky with which they "tied" the Sun, or constellations of stars, to their altars. In this way, they captured information delivered by powerful cosmic sources contained in the light. This was mostly done on dates that were important at the cosmic level. In addition to benefiting the communities and the land, this practice allowed the ancient apprentices and spiritual workers of the great *Wak'as* to live daily with the "captured" cosmic energies, through which the Universe helped them increase their wisdom.

Very near their *Wak'as*, through which our ancestors invoked the great universal powers, they constructed terraces and planted food. The leaves of edible plants, like the altars, served to capture light that was full of cosmic instructions. The plants received their power directly from the light of the sky, and also from the *Wak'a* itself, so that those who ate them received a combination of sacred nutrients that came from both sources. In those days, people who went to that type of *Wak'a* for learning purposes did not read books as is done in modern universities. Their "books" were what they ate, powerful varieties of corn, potatoes, *kiwicha*, *kañiwa*, quinoa, and many other plants.

Those wise ancestors learned not only to work the earth but also to work for the Earth as guardians of her memory. For many generations, they were dedicated to the task of tying the different solar cycles to their altars, and by doing so they maintained the memory and the awareness of how the Universe has been forming life over long periods of time. Generations of wise people "tied" the solar cycles of a year—of hundreds and even thousands of years—to their altars, temples, and lands, forming a necklace of time periods in which no cycle was disconnected from another. They anchored and stored the cosmic information that came from each cycle to live with them permanently, and in this way they never lost track of their own formation as beings of the Earth. Those who lived together with altars used for "tying the Sun" developed the capacity to bring their consciousness to these center points in which all the moments whose particular influences have formed the world were anchored and stored. Standing in this sacred place of cosmic memory, they became informed (formed from within) and loaded with instructions and updates. Since the Universe is in permanent growth and expansion, experiencing evolution and changes, it becomes indispensable for the Earth, and for us, to continually receive updates.

21

To Distribute Light
and Food

❖

The ancients knew that our energy comes from the Sun and our body from the Earth, and so they considered themselves the children of both. Just as every child resembles their parents, they understood that it was in our destiny to become like our father, a Sun, or like our mother, an Earth, who carries a little molten Sun in its center. The most developed of our Andean ancestors were considered children of the Sun because, after they had succeeded in storing a great quantity of solar energy in their bodies, they were able to crystalize small Suns within (in the case of men) or a Sun plus a Moon within their wombs (in the case of women). Far from being symbolic, this is based on something quite real since Father Sun gave them the light with which their inner light content grew, and Mother Earth gave them bodies capable of receiving, digesting, storing, refining, and sharing light.

When the most developed *Runa* worked with light, it was not just for their personal benefit. As members of communities, aware of being part of a greater body, they learned to distribute the sacred power that they stored. Each time it was important to accomplish works for the maintenance of their territories, they shared the power of their light, benefiting the greater population and the natural sources of life that sustained them. The large content of light shining in the interiors of some leaders ended up overflowing and watering everything around them—thus all that they touched with their energy grew to blossom and bear fruit. The material-spiritual leaders of antiquity made sure their communities did not suffer from poverty and that they had enough to live well. To generate material abundance in a world where money did not exist, they used everything that they had worked to develop. They used their practical knowledge, their *Munay* (will of the heart), their integrity, their unfailing reciprocity, the magnetism generated by their unification of their internal parts, their love for the Earth, their expressions of gratitude, their relationship with the sky, and the unity that, using their *Kuyay* (tender affection), they helped generate among the members of the land, the community, and the nation to which they belonged.

The sons and daughters of the Sun were able to move energies and to move the waters, and they made sacred power circulate in a vast world. This placed them at a higher level of leadership since their service to the people and to nature was sustained by a great natural power that lived in their interior. They created unity where there could have been separation, integrating the energies and experiences of the Earth and its inhabitants when they might have been dispersed and fragmented. This work was done because our *Pachamama* also has a body that receives and stores universal light, and exposed constantly to the variety of influences that the cosmos brings, it can also become decentered. Just like us, the Earth frequently needs *Walthay* (the centering of energies) to maintain its equilibrium. In antiquity, *Walthay* was done for the Earth through the use of *Wankas* (standing stones) and *Wak'as* that were placed at different locations within a vast territory, and it was done through ceremonies and offerings conducted simultaneously in all these locations, connected and integrated like a web. Since before the time of the *Inkas* and *Qollas*, ancient people knew how to weave invisible lines of energy called *Seq'e*. These lines, which united different sacred places, were widely used in the time of the *Inkas* and *Qollas* to distribute the cosmic light that they stored, refined, prayed over, and charged with intention. This light was distributed toward any place in need of help, places affected by drought, an epidemic, or some other natural disaster. And during times free of any emergency, the *Seq'es* (*Seq'ekuna* in

Quechua) simply served to nourish the world by distributing light charged with instructions along the vast net of *Wak'as*, the places where sacred energy could be deposited and from which it could be radiated when necessary. Depending on the power of a *Wak'a*, its radius of influence could be more or less extensive, at times benefiting only the territory where it was located and at other times reaching the entire Andean-Amazonian world, as was the case for the *Wak'a* called *Koriqancha* situated in the navel of the city of Cusco, a city in the shape of a Puma.

The wise custom of distributing light in a way similar to the way the human body distributes nutrients through its blood—and energy through the channels known as meridians in Chinese medicine—was essential in our ancestral culture. In the area of Cusco, ceremonies were conducted in very powerful places, such as *Koriqancha*, *Q'enqo*, and *Saqsaywaman*, where the great *Inka* and *Qolla* priests tied the content of cosmic energy drawn from the sky to their powerful altars and then distributed them throughout their world. Just as there were paths for public servants to travel and distribute the light contained in food and other material goods, so there were invisible paths to distribute pure energy. And just as there were places to deposit and keep the different types of material goods, called *Qolqa*, there were also places to deposit and keep the sacred, called *Wak'a*. These systems of distributing and storing for redistribution, parallel and complementary, assured the health of our ancestors' world. They were accustomed to constantly transferring food from one "sacred pot" to another in such a way that all the "pots" remained filled with all that was necessary for the people to live satiated at every level of their being. Their bodies were well-informed thanks to what fed them, filled with natural instructions that became extremely necessary, especially when cosmic cycles ended and the times changed. These instructions helped them to adapt to the changes without having to suffer too much.

FOURTH DOOR

❖

THE GIFT OF TIME

22

ADAPTING TO THE CHANGE
IN THE TIMES

❖

For the Earth and its inhabitants, the instructions that the Universe sends inviting us to participate in its order come through our closest star, the Sun, ruler of time and "the times." The continual movement of the Earth in relation to the Sun generates time. When I say "the times," I am referring not only to the changes of seasons but also to great cycles that come, go, and return caused by the movement of the Sun in relation to the rest of the stars. In Quechua, we call both time and space "*Pacha.*" Time-Space, or *Pacha*, acts as the container of our life experience. Like a moving home that transforms itself in accordance with the movement of the celestial spheres, *Pacha* often brings us to new cosmic spaces and alignments that create unknown opportunities for us.

We call the great spirit of *Pacha*, our Mother Time-Space, "*Pachamama*" (and when we refer specifically to the physical part of the land, we use the word "*Hallpa*" or "*Hallpamama*"). In the body of our *Pachamama*, time and space cannot be separated, for in our culture we are accustomed to seeing them simultaneously so as not to lose sight of their balance. Our houses, for example, have a space aspect to them and a time aspect, just like farms, mountains, jungles, and all the spaces we inhabit. All these spaces change when night comes or when dawn arrives. They change with the coming of summer or winter, and they change much throughout the years. Aware of these natural changes, we have to change as well in order to adapt. For example, our eyes help us to see in the daylight, and when it gets dark, we develop our night vision.

During the year there are times when we perform activities and rituals that help cultivate our food according to the nourishment it receives from the rain. And other times, without clouds when it does not rain, it becomes easy to watch the sky and acquire knowledge and wisdom by observing the stars, the times of *Pachakamaq* (the principle of the ordering of the Universe that complements *Pachamama*). There are different types of time, and in farming communities we have learned that for things to go well, we have to do our activities in their natural time, during the time of year they correspond to. Unfortunately, this healthy way of life is being lost. Now that so many people live in big cities, where they do not grow their own food and where the artificially illuminated night blocks the possibility of watching the movements of the stars, the modern world has become more like a factory. The times chosen to do things are produced by industrial agendas and technological capability, not by nature. The industrial world, no longer in sync with the rhythms of nature, has lost its way, its timing, and has become dull and clumsy, without the skill needed to adapt to the changing times. In reality, we don't even have sufficient collective awareness about the need to adapt ourselves to new times. There is only the habit of adapting ourselves to new technologies created by big business.

Traditional farmers who are not industrialized, from whom the world has much to learn, are accustomed to performing their activities at the proper moment in accord with the dictates of nature. As my brother Bacilio says, "During the season when it should rain, we play the *quena* (the Andean vertical flute) so that energy moves from above to below, and during the time when it should not rain, we play the *zampoñas* (reed pan pipes) and the *pututos* (conch shell trumpets) so that the breath of the musician travels from below upward." But now, with the growth of the tourist industry and because visitors want to learn about our culture in a short time, songs and dances with *zampoñas* have been turned into a spectacle performed in both the rainy and dry seasons. The same thing happens with the *quenas*, which are played at all times, even on days when it should not rain. In his own words, my brother says that the weather has become very confused because of our activities, and now it rains when it shouldn't, and it doesn't rain when it should. Sometimes, the farm is already sown with seeds, ready to receive water, and one must wait for months. And then, when the rains do finally come, it rains with such force that everything is ruined. This happened rarely in the past, but in the last few years it has become common.

Bacilio has also spoken about having been invited to participate in the celebration of World Water Day, which bothered him because those who created this initiative somewhere in Europe had not consulted with Andean farmers to choose the date. The date they chose was not good because it was the exact date that rain should have stopped in the Andes so that excess water would not ruin the ripe crops and because it was the time set aside to clean the land. This was in complete contradiction to our usual practices, and the only way to join with this good cause for nature was to call for water out of season and do something contrary to nature.

That which the modern world calls "the environment"—the source of water, air, and food—can also be called by its full name, "*Pachamama*," Mother Time-Space, so that we pay attention to the fact that when we cause her harm, we are harming both her space and her time. The human activities of the modern world not only contaminate and destroy our spaces but also fabricate times and rhythms of life that are contrary to nature. Therefore, the good people who work today to repair damages to "the environment" must also consider repairing time since space and time do not exist separate from each other.

It is very risky to lose the ability to adapt to changes in time, when big cycles end and new ones begin, since the consequences can actually be fatal. Remembering once again the *Ayar* sisters and brothers mentioned before, we urgently need to invoke *Mama Rewe* and *Ayar Uchu* as life principles that bring us back to the wisdom needed to humbly recognize that we are inside a Universal body that is much bigger than us and that has movements and rhythms we need to be in sync with. *Ayar Uchu* invites us to dance with grace and elegance on the dates when the changes happen, like the beginning of the seasons and other important cosmic dates. And *Mama Rewe* provides us with the natural wisdom of the feminine so that we may think more slowly, making it possible to listen to and follow the small drum we carry in our hearts, played by the pulse of the Universe, inviting us to the fiesta of life, a fiesta of health and abundance to which we will never arrive on time if we remain asleep.

In times of great changes, we must prevent humanity from becoming unaware of what is happening in the natural world to which it belongs. But we find a great obstacle in the fact that now humanity thinks that nature belongs to us, just as one may believe that they own the garden at their house. Actually, even that small garden belongs to the Universe, and it has a relationship with enormous stars moving across the sky that influence its life and its health. As a child, my grandmother used to tell us that instead of always looking down to search for food like chickens, we had to learn to look up and in all directions. Like eagles and owls, we had to pay attention to what moved in the distance, where that which feeds our food comes from, and make ourselves aware of what time would bring us.

WHAT TIME BRINGS US

❖

More powerful than the arrival of the rainy season or the dry season will be the arrival of a time that will offer conditions of life that are totally different from what we are accustomed to due to changes occurring in the positions of the stars in the sky. In order to recover our ability to recognize such cosmic events and to become aware of the change that approaches, we need to go back a few centuries to the moment in which memory was lost. Severe damage was inflicted on our relationship with time in the ancient European world when the original calendars, considered to be of pagan origin, were replaced by the Gregorian calendar. In ancient times, all over the world there were community celebrations that took place on those important dates when Mother Earth experiences an alignment with some cosmic event that could favor or put in danger the production of food and the health of the people. On these special dates, in addition to singing and dancing, the people made offerings and petitions to the sacred powers. Communities became fully aware of nature's rhythms, and dancing with them was one of the ways to become adapted to them. Without thinking of the damage this might cause, the original dates of these ceremonial encounters with the cosmic events were changed, or their real names were replaced with the names of saints, so that over time their original meaning was forgotten. I imagine that from then onward, the original communities that existed in the forests of Europe were no longer able to continue being instructed by nature at the times of the most important cosmic events. They were no longer able to synchronize themselves with the periodic changes that happen in *Pachamama*. They could no longer receive, through the art of praying together with mountains, trees, and wild animals on the sacred dates, the natural wisdom of the land where they lived, and so they were left out of paradise. By losing communication with the sacred powers of nature, ignorance grew in these communities, and people became dependent on "truths" that came from human authorities who spoke in the name of God or intellectual authorities who presented themselves as the only ones with true knowledge, while others were supposedly ignorant due to lack of religious or academic indoctrination.

Dependence on those who speak with religious, political, or intellectual authority prevails in modern society, and many individuals have not yet reclaimed their birthright to be in direct connection with sources of truth. But this is beginning to change. The time of supremacy of unconsciousness was produced during a long cosmic cycle that obligated humanity to pass through very difficult tests. But today the changing times favor the awakening of humanity. This is demonstrated by the fact that, all over the world, a desire is increasing to grow our ability to be in direct relationship with the true sources of what happens in our lives—cosmic, natural, and spiritual sources. It would not surprise me if soon we all return to wanting to use calendars that reflect the true rhythms of nature to which we belong.

The illusion of those who live in these industrialized times, damaged and distorted, has its roots in the belief that we are advancing, in the belief that humanity progresses as times goes on thanks to sophisticated technological development and enormous productivity. In reality, for a long time the dominant culture throughout the world has been lost, disconnected from the source, and centered on humans as if we were the source. Proud of what it has become, humanity cannot remember its original path, the one laid out by the stars, that the ancients saw in sacred fires and water mirrors. Modernity has been sustained by technological advances more than by the internal development of humanity. There are people in what are considered the developed countries, able to send spaceships to other planets, who still believe that the year begins on the first of January. True modernization will occur when the movements of humanity return to being a part of the rhythm of the Universe; when what constitutes reality ceases to be designed only by humans, according to our convenience; when people rediscover a proper relationship with *Pachamama* and stop destroying the natural sources of their own food; when we regain the ability of communicating with beings and natural powers in order to better the climate; and when understanding how things work stops being so complicated and becomes something simple as it was in the time of our first ancestors thousands of years ago. As everything moves in circles, returning to the beginning as it advances, the new modernity will meet and be greatly influenced by ancestral wisdom.

There are changes in the world that are produced by human initiatives and changes that the Universe produces through cosmic events. At some point, change-provoking cosmic events always end up manifesting through powerful social movements. It would be wonderful if the repair to the damage done to time was coming from a movement initiated by humanity, but if not, it will still happen. A natural revolution is coming now that we are arriving at the completion of a certain circular movement of stars closely related to the Earth. In Quechua, we use the word "*Pachakuti*" to name the moment of completion of a long cosmic cycle that coincides with the beginning of a new one. In our culture, we understand that, because everything in the Universe moves in circles, the possibility exists that very ancient times can return to become our future. With their qualities and potential enriched through their long cosmic journey, these ancient times return when the stars return to the same place in the sky where they were found thousands of years ago.

PACHAKUTI, THE TIME OF THE BIG RETURN

❖

In the word "*Pachakuti,*" "*Pacha*" means "time," and "*Kuti*" means "return" or "turn." Thanks to our ancestors, who observed the sky for thousands of years, we understand that right now we are at the beginning of a new cycle, a new *Pachakuti.* According to what our ancestors observed, a *Pachakuti* that brings prosperity follows one that brings enormous difficulties. Then comes another bringing prosperity, and so on. We understand that the one beginning now, fortunately, brings the conditions whereby humanity can recover from its amnesia and the self-destructive behavior in which it has been stuck for some time.

With all respect for those who think that history appears to be a train that never stops moving forward and rolls on leaving everything behind, interpreting reality from my own Andean worldview, I can say that time instead moves in circles and that it's possible that a wave of ancestral memory may be coming to unblock the flow of what has been interrupted. I strongly feel in my heart the possibility of recovering ourselves, the possibility of returning to being wise humans like our ancestors were, with the capacity to ensure the continuation of our existence. I see that things are changing and that we are now finding the door to an expansive, luminous space, full of new possibilities and ancient knowledge. I believe we are going to learn to repair the damage that has been done to Mother Earth and that we will remember how to live calm, satisfied, physically and spiritually satiated lives, without ambitions that would cause us to continue doing harm. Informed and instructed by the Sun and other beings in nature, we can finally become free from the anxiety that the mind suffers when it does not know how to confront something difficult and unknown. By revaluing and respecting the Indigenous communities that kept the seeds of food and wise culture since remote times, we can return to producing an abundance of natural food and medicines, as well as the food that our spirits need to be able to recuperate from having lived for so long in a world that didn't nourish them.

I felt the moment when the *Pachakuti* arrived. Something woke me very early on the day of the winter solstice. It was very cold, and even before I could see it, the Sun made me walk through the fields toward the east so that I could watch it come up while standing in a sacred space near my house. When the Sun rose, it filled me with light, and I knew, without any doubt, that it was a new Sun. Its power made me feel like when one takes a bath in freezing water, submerged in a lake, more awake than ever. Inside me, everything was renewed, and I felt like a newborn, ready to participate in a harvest greater than has ever been seen.

Our beloved *Pachamama* is made of space and time, and so as we work to harvest what was sown in space, we may also be able to harvest what has been sown in time. It is up to us to harvest that which our ancestors seeded so abundantly, thinking of us, their descendants, in this time of great fertility in which the new Sun is bringing us good news related to a real possibility for unblocking our original cultures. And will it happen that everything that becomes liberated from the interruption produced by colonialism returns to expand with great fluidity? Will it be that, once unblocked, the wisdom of the past will put its ancestral mark on new things? It would be wonderful if all the spaces that the modern world considers "archaeological sites" recover their vitality so that they can serve to receive and shelter the gifts of a new time. It would be wonderful if they could become living houses of the sacred, used once again for the original purposes for which they were constructed. From mysterious spaces filled with black light that exist in our *Wak'as*, I hear ancient songs reemerge, an old yet familiar vibration returning to refresh our tired modern world. I see an ancient past infusing the present with its universal, eternal wisdom so that the modern culture, today anxious to innovate, not be reinvented by human imagination or by something artificial but rather by the sacred breath of something real and natural. In times when our lives are in danger, we should not be guided by new illusions produced by the evolution of our imagination but by original instructions provided by the Earth and the Universe. And I know that if we wait patiently, the instructions will come because that's what happened to people from other times of beginning. It happened to our own ancestors, the ones who knew how to be in silence for entire nights, listening to the star-filled sky. Using the ceremonial arts that lead us to listen with our whole being, we can receive help to decide what we need to do, and we will no longer need to suffer, trying to do something without the guidance of the heart of the great body inside of which we have always been.

The *Pachakuti* that began five hundred years ago, coinciding with the European invasion, brought very difficult times for our Andean-Amazonian populations. What arrives now is bringing us opportunities so that we may flourish again as owners of our own destiny, as people directly in charge of our health and the happiness of our communities.

In addition to being the end of a short cycle of five hundred years, this moment also marks the end of a longer cycle that has been going on for thousands of years, affecting all of humanity. We know then that the gifts the new light is bringing at the beginning of this new cycle are not coming only for the patient Andean-Amazonian peoples but for all of humanity across the Earth. Right now, the change in the climate caused by humankind happens alongside a change in the light caused by the beginning of this new cosmic cycle. Everything that lives on Mother Earth must adapt to both changes. The survival and continuation of the human race depends not only on the climate. It also depends on the light of this new Sun and the way it provokes a reactivation of our collective ancient memory. Remembering the original design for good living, we can return to being authentic *Runa*, people with influence in the healthy state of the world. With our skillful way of feeding the sacred, we may occupy anew the role that corresponds to us in nature. And I have heard some say that perhaps the Earth would be better without us, but I cannot agree because we also are part of the Earth, members of her body, and we have an important function to fulfill. And in any case, what mother wants to lose a son or a daughter?

During this powerful moment of starting again, which will last for decades, the boundary line between the material world and the spirit world will remain thin and easy to cross because a lot of energy will have to travel from one side to the other. The work of forming the new humanity goes together with the repair of the damage done to life on Earth. Many dreams will come to us from the spirit world, and many of them, over time, will come true. Each nation on Earth will have its own work to do. Here, we who are the descendants of the Indigenous on this continent now called America will have the task of calling upon our ancestors, the ones who knew how to listen to light and to breathe light. Through our own awakening we can help them be freed from that which interrupted the continuity of their marvelous culture, and being back in touch with them will help us recover our memory. As my wife, Marilyn, once told me after coming out of a powerful ceremony, we need to go back to our roots, and from that ancient past our future will begin. Those of us who were born in the Andean-Amazonian world, inheritors of ancient mother-cultures such as those from Caral, Chavin, and Tiwanaku, need to reclaim the ancient wisdom that continued being transmitted during no less than five thousand years, up until the time of the *Inkas* and the European invasion. Surprisingly, some of the original features of these mother-cultures and of the culture of hundreds of sovereign nations that were influenced by them continue to be present in our way of being. In many communities, we have inherited customs that form an essential part of our way of living and working, among which stands highest the custom of preparing offerings to feed the sources of our food. But sadly, the influence of the ancestral cultures in our lives has been diminishing every day because it had to compete for five hundred years with ideologies full of falsehoods that impeded the free distribution of original wisdom. During all that time, claiming our inheritance didn't feel as possible as it does now. And now, those of us who do really want to claim it celebrate the arrival of this new *Pachakuti* that comes to give us the chance to unblock ourselves, and so we may recover our memory. When reflecting on the recent findings of the Peruvian archaeologist Ruth Shady and her colleagues, it would be wonderful if answers were given to our burning questions. How was it possible, more than five thousand years ago, for the people of the oldest civilization on the American continent—the people of Caral who inhabited the central coast of Peru—to become a mother-culture of so many other cultures of the Andean-Amazonian world without using war as a means of conquest? What talents did they have? Where were their roots planted? What made them capable of developing a culture whose influence and ramifications still do not die, even six thousand years later despite the conquest? What were the hearts of those men and women like? How did they talk? How did they sing? Where did so much wisdom come from?

❖

Something is moving us from within as the power of the Universe moves the spiral, bringing us back to the center, where all energy receives the impulse to elevate. Now, at the beginning of this *Pachakuti*, I hear these instructions: "The center of the Earth can be anywhere you are standing or sitting. Instead of seeing the center of the Earth as a dot in flat space, try to see it as a tube of light that goes through the planet and extends, without limit, to the rest of the Universe. Then feel what happens when you stand in this tube of light, which quickly transports you back to the origin. Suddenly you are elevated, you feel peace, you feel more at home than ever, in a luminous place where you know, without any doubt, that it is you who has the power to take care of the world. Still, and yet with your mind moving through a vast world full of infinite different places, you can be the caretaker of all that your awareness can hold. And you can enjoy what happens when everything flows together, toward your center, and becomes one in the one who is looking— inside yourself. Feeling what the ancestors felt when they did the same maneuver, you can already remember and recover the greatness of their world—so abundant, fertile, and full of possibilities—which was not Caral, or Cusco, or Peru. It was nothing short of all the terrestrial space that serves to contain the light.

"Before the people of this present time, there were those who knew who they were, to whom the Universe to which they belonged gave everything they needed, including the light of their happiness. Those people who lived simultaneously in the material and spirit worlds recognized themselves as sons and daughters of the Earth, grandchildren of the stars, and great-grandchildren of the galaxy. They recognized the Sun, a child of the constellations, as their father. Called to participate in the expansion of the Universe, Father Sun joined with beautiful Mother Earth to have generations of children, small terrestrial stars, the *Runa*, destined to ascend and return to the origin of the energy that animates them from within. This light that in the beginning descended from the center of our galaxy, enriched by the human experience, is turning around to go back. That energy in motion lives in the spirits of the *Runa*, and your ancestors knew this. Today the spiral, about to expand, brings you to the center and wakes you up, calling you to be ready. Here, it will kill what you are not, preparing your spirit to start again, intact and grown up. And you will be able to continue in the new cycle, ascending and returning without realizing it, while you recover the art of living with awareness, the art of good living."

HARVESTING RICHES
OF THE PAST

❖

The new does not take away the old. This new time needs the past, needs the memory of what happened through thousands of years, so that we may benefit from the wisdom that only life experience on Earth produces. It would not work to our benefit if, while welcoming a new cycle, we simply discarded the memory of the path we traveled to get here and the possibility of giving thanks, of knowing to whom we owe gratitude. Feeling rejuvenated and empowered by the new opportunities offered to us by the Universe and being freed from the tightness of our old clothes should not make us forget or fail to appreciate where we come from.

The mummies of the great *Inkas*, like that of the Inka Pachakutiq himself, lived in full view of the people in the city of Cusco, and anyone could stop by to greet them and talk to them. Similarly, it was common for people to keep at least the skull of their grandparents in their homes, open to view, so that they would not forget them and so they would keep their relationship with them alive. In this way, the past lived in the everyday life of the present. And it will continue to do so, for as long as we continue using the Quechua word "*Ñaupa*." In the Quechua language, the word "*Ñaupa*" links space and time in a very specific way. "*Ñaupa*" means "the space in front of us" and also means "time past." Therefore, for a speaker of Quechua to be looking to the front and to be facing the past are the same. And so, it is said that we Quechua speakers walk backward with our backs to the future. Step by step, like walking backward without seeing the future that is behind us, we see the past grow. In front of us, time-space keeps getting bigger and bigger and becomes the wide and generous field where we reap our cultural riches. Step by step, flowing backward, we live with humility, giving thanks for everything we have inherited, relaxed, without distrust for the stones in the road, with no interest in conquering the future.

Those of us who grew up in the Andean culture feel joy in finding in the past a field full of produce to harvest, especially the fruits of experience, the wisdom of our ancestors, and the energy that emanates from their traces, which are engraved in their works, and in the breath of their songs. To the contrary, modern culture only trusts in innovation as the source of prosperity and considers the past to be the source of something backward and primitive. And this makes me question how much modern culture feels the need to break up with the past.

Nowadays, our ancient culture, even while seen as interesting and even fascinating for some, does not have an appeal for most people. To live in a culture marked by the significance of the word "*Ñaupa*" must cause a lot of discomfort to those who do not want to have the past in front of them, who have a past they prefer to not look at, from which they try to flee. For all the inherited trauma that exists, many people prefer to look for better lives in an imaginary future and therefore prefer to live in a society that promises such a thing. Being the kind of people who look toward "a better future," they tend to think that inhabitants of Andean communities will always be poor because of us not being very interested in conquering the future, lacking ambition. Instead, those who understand that this way of being actually makes us rich can say they really understand our culture. The world we have in front of us belongs to us. It belongs to us in the sense that we own the responsibility of taking care of everything that has already grown, everything to which we belong, that we feel affection for, and everything that our ancestors created. Thanks to this, we cannot consider our grandmother poor as she walks barefoot along a mountain path, carrying an enormous bundle. Because she belongs to the mountain, and the mountain belongs to her, as do all the mountains around her whose names she calls when offering them the coca leaves that she puts in her mouth. And the lakes are hers, as are the springs, the rivers, the clouds, and all the birds whose names she knows. She behaves like "the owner" of the world but not as its proprietor, more as someone who cares for and nourishes it. She, the owner, has great influence on her world, simply with her presence, and even more so when she prays and gives thanks. She doesn't care much about accumulating a fortune to build a mansion. Rather, she prefers to be outside in the infinitely large home of nature. Nor does she wish to get entertainment from a screen because she always has something marvelous to look at. Some days, there are sunsets where she passes through invisible doors. A blue wind carries her to places very few have seen, places where a marvelous past, crystalized for eternity by her ancestors, opens roads for her to sacred hiding places where she is brought to play like when she was a child. On her feet, painted black by the earth—cracked, worn, powerful—one sees maps drawn of the marvelous places she has visited, sometimes hungry, sometimes cold, sometimes ecstatic. She, who some people call poor, possesses immeasurable wealth.

Some of her grandchildren, for whom she represents the past that they have been told to flee, prefer white sneakers instead of our traditional sandals made of rubber tires that we call *ojotas*. With those white sneakers, they imagine they could quickly run away and, one day, become like famous North American basketball players who, being descended from our African brothers who were also enslaved, are now famous millionaires. And good for them if they do. But how many grandchildren leave their communities in search of work (at times they have no other option) or in search of riches and end up suffering in the big cities amid a tenacious struggle to one day feel accepted as part of the society of poor people who have white sneakers and cars, the society of those that didn't stay to receive their inheritance from thousands of years of culture and from the times in which the stars were born and the mountains grew and the seas were filled? Converted into poor city people with big aspirations, they end up knowing other types of hunger, some insatiable, always occupied by trying to have more than they already have and no longer able to be in contemplation with a mountain, receiving the world, the wind, the deepest rest.

Understandably, there are people in other cultures who think that we cause harm to children if they are not given, through education, the opportunity of becoming this type of poor person with the capacity to accumulate things. In societies where material prosperity stands as the highest goal, the children receive education so that they may have a chance to move forward and conquer the future. And if they come from the Indigenous world, the antiquity that was their inheritance and their wealth becomes a history class, and the playground and learning spaces of their grandparents become documentaries. While starving their deepest being, they have no other choice but to get used to living without stopping, always trying to get something, with anxiety. The intense competition with others who are also running toward a better future creates a fear of ending up being crushed in this race that resembles a stampede of bulls. It never allows one to stop and rest like those who can trust in all the help they receive just by breathing.

I can understand the great resistance, generated over time, to wanting to look at the past with gratitude or simply to look at what is in the past. The profound wounds of those who have been run over—and of those who run over—have created generations of people who walk in this world loaded with trauma, resentments, guilt, and shame that they have inherited. The modern world seems condemned to continue being a society of people running toward the future, escaping the past, pursuing what they imagine they can have, even when they already have enough or even too much. As we can all see, most people nowadays, after getting what they desire, only continue wanting to have more. Because deep down they are filled with an endless poverty. We can all see also how this human condition continues to create a way of life with a very high cost that depletes people's energy at the same rate it depletes the riches of nature. And really, becoming super rich doesn't seem to be the solution. The sensation of not having enough also lives in very large mansions, together with the fear or even the terror produced by just thinking about the possibility of losing what has been accomplished through so much work. Who wants to end up feeling unprotected, being less than others?

Valuing the old customs, taking advantage of an ancient wisdom while looking at ourselves through the mirror of our ancestors, some of us still prefer to continue producing the wealth that can never be lost, the wealth that dwells in *Ñaupa*. For there is so much for us to harvest from the times in which we planted the seeds of the good relationships we have: the love of relatives, countrymen, friends, wise ancestors, powerful spirits, mountains, lakes, rivers, and stars.

It does feel good when those who have left and who have been away for a time without their mountains and their community return to receive their share of the endless harvest. Even more, sometimes they return with useful knowledge, with important things they learned in the big city. In such cases, we see that it was worth the sacrifice since these relatives have the ability to better the lives of our people and open their eyes to things they didn't know, among them the true origin of the deceptions they normally suffer, deceptions created by those who, from tall buildings in the big cities, have control over the national economic projects that never consider deeply enough the distribution of wealth and the well-being of all. On the other hand, those who return to the wisdom of the community receive the enormous benefit of being helped to remember that at times it rains a lot and at others just a little, and that at times there is much of what is needed and at others only a little. Because nature works that way. Wisdom returns to us when remembering that the way of nature does not make us poor, because we are experienced people who know how to prevent shortages, how to adapt ourselves to changing times, and how to be happy without lots of material possessions. Wisdom returns to us when remembering the true meaning of poverty. In Quechua, the word "*Wakcha*" translates as "poor," and this word does not refer to a person who does not have enough material goods; it refers to a person who doesn't have people to turn to, not having a community. We are only poor when we do not have time, especially the time to cultivate the good relationships we have with those who will never forget us. And we would be really poor if we also forgot our ancestors and the great treasures they planted, counting on us to gather the harvest.

26

THE ART OF SEEING
THE FUTURE

❖

The world rotates and receives new times the way a ship in motion receives new undulations from the sea at every moment. If the sea represents time and the ship represents space, on which part of the ship do we place leaders and spiritual workers who attempt to see into the future? On the prow, of course. On the prow, there isn't enough room for many people. In our communities, we are used to having only a few leaders and spiritual workers standing there, looking at the future, confronting the mystery, looking in the distance for a place to arrive or to return (*Pachakuti*). The rest of the people, traveling like crewmembers on the boat, are not so much interested in that type of duty. They are busy looking in the opposite direction, contemplating the *Ñaupa* (past times/ space in front of them). With their attention focused on the path that has already been traveled, they continue weaving the culture. The culture of a people does not originate from what the leaders decide as much as it does from what the people choose not to forget. The people know how to select what must not be forgotten and the flavors they want to continue savoring.

In stable times, without great social changes or severe natural disasters, our ancestors continued weaving their cultures from the threads of the past, harvesting the fruits of their experiences and of the experiences of those who lived before them, selecting the best seeds to leave something of value to their descendants. The art of seeing the future was reserved for a small number of individuals and became really important when times of great change approached. In those times, some knowledge of what was coming became necessary in order to be prepared and to have the wisdom to make the best decisions. Those who knew how to read the stars, the seers and the guardians of the oracular *Wak'as*, lived with a type of intensity that was incomprehensible for others. They required great abilities to be able to anticipate what time was bringing, and those individuals had to return to the village frequently to live simple lives among the people. Otherwise, loneliness, fatigue, or power could destroy them.

In our Indigenous communities, we still have customs inherited from that ancient wisdom. And we well know that the visionary leaders, putting themselves out front, experience the arrival of difficult times before others since they are the first to see them. They and the people closest to them always end up being the first to suffer the impact, but they also have the fortune of being the first to receive cosmic, earthly, and spiritual instructions and know how to adapt, survive, and grow in the face of natural adversities that accompany the changing of the times. What was never easy was passing the understanding of what was happening to the rest of the people. Some conflict arises from the fact that, after long periods of stability, many people become conservative or "traditionalists" and tend to react in unfriendly manners toward those who look toward the future and see new things coming. True seers, star readers, and gifted spiritual workers, even when recognized as useful people, can meet with resistance among their people and occasionally be subject to forms of mistreatment when the news they bring causes turmoil.

To me it seems strange that it has become fashionable in the modern world to be a shaman, while in our communities this has never been the case. Why would so many individuals want to leave the tranquility of their simple human lives to become these intense and strange types of leaders? I don't know if they understand that they will have to frequently make the sacrifice to stop enjoying the beautiful panorama of *Ñaupa*, all that already exists that they know and live with, to turn around, face the future, and embark on the difficult task of trying to see what may be there in the unknown. I am surprised that there are so many people interested in performing this role since it requires abandoning the known surface of the human world and journeying to dark depths to encounter what is there to be seen. In there, illuminated by black light, there may be something new wanting to be born or something ancient wanting to return. If someone wants this vision in order to inform their people, I can understand. But why are there now so many individuals who want to do this kind of difficult work? After much reflection, I see that this is because, during a *Pachakuti* (the beginning of a new cycle), the times are far from stable, and this changes what people normally do. Great changes arrive, one after the other, and in times like these, each one wants to assume leadership of their own life and of their family. Cosmic nature herself is waking up millions of people so that they can "see" for themselves where the road is heading. It makes sense that during times of emergency, when the alarm has sounded, all the crewmembers on the ship want to turn around and look ahead to the front just as the star readers and those who the modern world calls shamans do.

Humanity today seems so lost that there is a clear need to be able to trust in the help of good leaders—honest, wise, and prepared—such as good-hearted and skilled women seers and the experienced guardians of oracle *Wak'as*. On the other hand, it is understandable that so many individuals want to have their own vision and to be their own leaders since there has been such a lack of trustworthy leadership in the years leading up to this time of emergency. In my humble opinion, this tendency can find fertile ground on the spontaneous, intuitive, feminine side of humanity and can run into many stumbling blocks on the more rational masculine side. The masculine mind has the tendency to be slower at understanding things and would need many years of instruction and learning to be ready for meeting the challenges of these times. My brother Manari and other spiritual leaders for whom I have a lot of respect keep saying that, in this time of great change, the greatest responsibilities, in terms of leadership, will be held by women and those with a feminine mind.

27

In the Face of Danger, Don't Lose the Feminine

❖

Historical documents show how, in the time of the *Inkas*, when men went to war they were accompanied by their partners, women who stayed near the battlefield to attend to their wounds and to help them recover their hearts. And unless they were one of those born with the skill of being life-long warriors, after they recovered, the women took them back home, to the warmth of the community. Just as important as winning the battle was not losing the mental or emotional health of the community members.

In times of danger, and even more so when there already exists an accumulation of collective traumas caused by previous calamities, women, men, and communities tend to lose touch with their feminine side. The ancestors, conscious of this, tried to avoid it through encouraging a type of behavior based on the complements of masculine will and feminine caregiving. Women, with their tenderness, were dedicated to impeding the warrior will from becoming excessive. Even when it was respected and considered necessary for the protection of the people, the strong will of the warriors wasn't permitted to go too far, to a place where it would lose contact with the tender, affectionate relationships that bond members of a community. As they kept watch over the need to maintain the emotional health of their families, the hearts of their men, and a nonviolent environment for their children, the women conserved their own powerful femininity—and femininity was never devalued.

With a masculine will that wants to accomplish difficult goals and determined to overcome adversity, human societies tend to give priority to *doing*, leaving aside the needs of our *beings*, neglecting our feelings. And when strategic thinking becomes more important than feeling, intuition and other forms of feminine wisdom are lost. Creating an enormous contradiction, those who use their masculine will in this way, excluding feminine capacities, put their own people in even more danger since there is nothing more dangerous than launching ourselves against something much greater than ourselves without holding as much wisdom as possible. I wonder what would have happened if, when the Spanish came, the women had been the ones who led the resistance, and I am inclined to think that everything would have been very different. Manqo Inka, the main ruler at that time, acted with feminine wisdom when he invited Francisco Pizarro to enter Cusco as a guest and to be his friend. Unfortunately, he was too young to possess the vision and spiritual power of a mature, developed grandmother, and the Spanish ended up deceiving him.

Developing our masculine side helps us anticipate what is coming and prepare ourselves. Developing our feminine side, always related to the moment, gives us the power of flowing with whatever comes and without needing to know. Feminine people tend to flow in a natural way, and masculine people also have some of this ability because, since our births, we all learn to adapt to the weekly changes caused by the lunar cycles, changes that happen in the state of our body's waters, emotions, and dreams. Guided by our feminine sides, we can feel the natural flow of things and move with sufficient confidence, as when one moves with the current of a river. In the rapids of life, we can swiftly avoid the heavy obstacles imposed by our own agendas and come to our best actions, the ones we make with lightness and spontaneity. Our wonderful actions, a surprise even to ourselves, can save our lives when we respond well and without delay, without overthinking, to something unknown. And some situations, like Manqo Inka facing the invaders that came to destroy our world, teach us that sometimes having intuition may not be enough and that we also need the capacities of a well-developed grandmother: heart centered, clever, astute, quiet, observant, patient, unconditional, resilient, experienced, soft, and strong.

Adapting oneself quickly to something unknown requires flexibility and fluidity, feminine qualities of those who never stay stuck in their previous knowledge or waste time defending it. They have the ability to take measure of things that are in motion and changing, defying modern rationality. Despite having a quality of rigor with which it looks for evidence to support its hypotheses, modern rationality also has great limitations due to its lack of feminine attributes, its poor ability to adapt itself to the unexpected, its slow analytic thought processes, its doubts, and a complicated relationship with certainty. The heavy baggage of knowledge used as a reference to understand something ends up being an obstacle. One can observe, for example, the delay in accepting climate change as a crisis with fatal consequences among the world's scientific community when it had already required urgent attention for a long time.

To be alert in the face of danger does not require one to be afraid or alarmist; it only requires that one be attentive through feeling. All living beings can develop a state of alertness and the ability to know without the need for thinking. This feminine form of perception—intuitive, bodily, awake, like the sense of smell of a jungle creature—can be our greatest protection when facing danger. With an alert body, in sync with the heart of the Earth we walk on, we get to know what the Earth knows in the same way an animal knows something—with total certainty.

The feminine habit of synchronizing our life rhythms with the rhythms of nature, the way a *Runa* dances in sync with the music that moves her, helps us maintain our bodies and our minds in an elegant state of alertness. Signals that the body receives, the heart and the spirit understand (*Yuyay*). In order to know how to take advantage of the unique opportunities offered by the change in these times, we must develop the feminine capacity of foretelling possible dangers for the continuation of our existence. And then we must allow the masculine will to enter into action to assure, in harmony with our land, the production of food, access to water, and the safety of our children. Guided by feminine knowledge, we take urgent action when faced with dangers or threats. And only after having taken those actions and observing their consequences do we understand more fully what we have done. Thankful for having learned something, we then continue flowing in the next river that carries us. Wired to be this way, it is difficult for some of us to work with the methods of the modern world that insist on learning and understanding before taking action. We are more familiar with the way of thinking we call *Yuyay*, which happens during the action or when one reflects right after having performed the action. In the word "*Yuyay*," thinking, remembering, and understanding come to be the same. And it seems to me that in addition to referring to looking at *Ñaupa* and harvesting the experience of the past, *Yuyay* refers also to remembering the present, to be attentive to what is happening in the moment and recognizing all that came together to create the particular nature of the moment. In *Yuyay* thinking, understanding comes as a realization, as a revelation. To receive it, one must be free of anxiety, without the fear of not-knowing and truly uninterested in losing time trying to demonstrate what one knows.

❖

When a new time comes and something happens in the sky that creates a wave that threatens to bring destruction in order to liberate us from a place where we have been stuck for a long time, we respond, dancing with joy and without fear, with the present movement of time-space. We hear the universal "music" that is moving the Earth and simultaneously perform an act of power, through which we call together all our internal parts to move in accord. The entire community performs this same maneuver when it is called to gather, to reunite, and to integrate all its members on a specific date. In beautiful ceremonies and festivals, the unity of people that makes up our community succeeds in creating balance instead of falling when hit by a powerful cosmic event. Singing and dancing, we align ourselves with the moon, the equinoxes, the solstices, and all the events that move us from the sky without forgetting to welcome the beginning of great cosmic cycles like the one happening at just this moment.

8

The Sacred Time
of Total Fulfillment

❖

For all of us who live beneath the sky, something arrives just now, something like an enormous gift wrapped in light. But what can a gift be good for when we do not take the time to open it? Times like these, of new beginnings, require a different attitude from us because receiving becomes more important than doing. To open the gift, it is necessary to stop what we have been doing and pay much attention because inside the box the gift comes in, there is another box, and within that one another, and another.

Our problems are not going to be solved overnight, and our world is going to take some time to change, the time it takes us to stop doing things as we have been doing them so that we can carefully, with the curiosity of children, dedicate ourselves to opening the gifts the Universe is bringing. The new light arriving at dawn in these days and years of the new beginning brings us seeds that carry the memory of our future inside them, the possibilities we will live with from now on. The last box will open like a seed that has been well-planted and well-watered, and from it will grow the new landscape that our grandchildren will grow up in.

To realize this task, it will help to listen to those who have more experience listening. In many Indigenous communities all over the world, there are cultural practices and customs that offer the members of the community the opportunity to rest from their daily labors and to participate in rituals, ceremonies, and festivals that help them open themselves to receiving food and instruction from the light. I will share one example, told to me by a *Runa* of Cusco, my brother Bacilio Zea Sánchez, who once witnessed something magical in a community in Quillabamba that he was visiting. Bacilio said that after the people finished their daily tasks, someone shouted, "Let's tie the Sun!" and what the people did was stop time. Together, they stopped time to share the fullness of being. They sat down in a field to eat potatoes, corn, and beans and then chewed coca leaves while the only thought that was heard there was *"Hallpaykusunchis,"* which means "Let's be Earth—with tenderness—for our benefit." I learned to call this way of experiencing the present moment *Hawkay Pacha*, the time of total plenitude, of the fullness of being. Stopped time. On seeing that just as the present arrives, it becomes the past, the ancients learned to "tie the Sun" in order to stop time and make the state of plenitude last an eternal moment. In this way, they lengthened their lives while taking advantage of precious moments that also gave them the chance to receive food and light until they were fully satiated. We have been able to maintain these customs up until today. Without rushing, we sit to chew *Kuka* leaves together or to share some food, and just as also happens in our ceremonies, we find rest from doing, the profound rest called *Samay*, which means "to rest" and also "to breathe." In moments like this, we completely renew our energy, refresh our minds, open our hearts, and in the greatest simplicity enjoy ourselves. From our ancestors we learned to tie the Sun and stop time, to benefit from the "no time" in which we experience the most elevated states of our being. At times, there are many of us together when we experience being silenced by the great power of a sacred source of life. As it happened when we were babies and cried our lungs out to ask for milk from the breasts of our mothers, we are heard and become filled with light and vitality, completely satiated, satisfied, and so ecstatic that there could be nothing more we could want.

Marvelous experiences like the kind Bacilio shared with me happen frequently in remote places in the Andean world and the Amazon jungle, where communities live far from the various authorities that have existed since the time of colonization, places where the communities have not lost their connection to the wisdom of the Earth and where they still know how to receive food for the heart and instruction for the mind, which come from the Universe. Thanks to such communities, the memory of the true *Runa* has not been completely lost over the hundreds of years in which the forgetfulness of the conquistadors prevailed. Unlike the Indigenous who could continue living in their sacred lands, those that ended up living in cities and their descendants were educated and conditioned by punishment and reward to fear the good spirits that their grandparents had been feeding for centuries. Many generations have passed since Indigenous people were exposed to political authorities and religious colonizers here and in other countries of the world. Even in Europe, Indigenous Europeans began, at some point, to be punished for being what they were: people of the Earth, natural, beautiful, wild, and refined in their simple wisdom. Today, the majority of people find it hard to trust deeply in the ability to receive instructions directly from the Earth and from the universal light that our Father Sun shines on us. What was very easy for our ancestors has become difficult for most of us. When a large question or doubt arises, or a threat to the continuation of our existence emerges, many people turn to the opinion of someone famous, or they consult with a machine, instead of using their own antennae and their own hearts.

Humanity will need to regain its confidence in the ancient cultural practices that a few people have guarded for everyone, practices that help people be guided by their feelings, intuition, and dreams and to use communal counsel to filter out falsehoods until everyone can see the truth appear. One person, in isolation, can confuse a message from spirit or an instruction contained in light with their own fears and desires. But an entire community is not confused so easily, even more so if they use medicine and rituals that have the power to illuminate what one cannot see so easily.

Tired from living with mistrust and with a hunger for spiritual food, many individuals are returning to, and others are visiting for the first time, those who have kept the memory of the original *Runa* alive. It is becoming more common for people to seek an alternative to the modern way of doing things with the desire to learn and develop their own connections with sources of wisdom and to receive instructions directly from the Universe and the spirit world. For that very reason, many individuals today are seeking help from those who practice ancient Indigenous customs. With greater frequency, people from cities and people of European descent are participating in circles of Indigenous people. In these meetings and ceremonies, we share with those who visit us that there can be no meetings without spirit, especially if the meetings aim to find solutions, make decisions, or come to good agreements. Because if we leave out our spiritual side, we lose half of who we are and half of our capacity. Just as blood can only be seen when we bleed, spirit can only be seen when we pray. And so we must pray together. And by prayer I am referring to speaking from the heart, conducting ourselves with love and respect toward the sacred sources of life, calling with the elevated vibration of our sacred speech and songs to our allies in the spiritual world and to our own spirits to be present.

In our meetings with visitors from other cultures, we have realized that we cannot resolve our differences on the material plane because on that plane it is appropriate that we have differences so that we can complement each other. We can only resolve our differences on the spiritual plane where we are all the same. Therefore, it benefits us to carry out rituals so that, together, we pass from the material world to the spiritual. Similarly, we have seen that it does not help us very much to base our meetings on an agenda that has been written down on paper and that it serves us better to know what to ask for and to ask with humility, lighting a sacred fire, elevating a song, sharing our hearts. And as a wise grandmother once told me and my family, "We have to have patience as we do these works because the deepest things need time to come to the surface." We have to give ourselves at least a few days in front of a sacred fire to continue asking before one begins to feel clearly the presence of what has been called for: our own presence, ourselves reunited as wise spirits who generate the medicines that our damaged material world needs.

EPILOGUE

❖

"To have good health, use your *Munay*. To not be sick, care for the Earth. Take care of the Earth, from which your 'sacred pot' was made. Your 'sacred pot' not only holds your content. Many things are happening inside it, and something is being cooked. Sooner or later, what is happening inside you will produce the delight of your being. Then, do not forget to care for your 'sacred pot.' Pay attention to see if it is scraped on one side or if it has a small hole somewhere. Take care not to allow something to enter your contents that can make you sick. Such things can happen to anyone at any moment. A chance accident or some collective illness from the family, the community, or the nation can harm your 'sacred pot.' Take care to learn to fix it yourself each time something goes wrong, keeping out of harm's way what lives inside. And if you have any influence in your family, your community, or your nation, help those large 'sacred pots' that contain them remain healthy, solid, and beautiful.

"Your *Munay* makes you pay constant attention, not to what they say on television but to what you perceive directly with your own senses and feelings. Observe signals that nature offers you and decide whether to continue on or to stop and make corrections before continuing. If difficulties follow you, tell them to a stone and then throw the stone into a river so it can take them away. When a sign tells you that something undesirable awaits you a little up ahead, just stop and then spin leftward to make a complete circle. In this way, you can nullify the direction and ask time to be generous and to take you by some other path to find what you truly want, something really good for you and your people. Everything begins with your will, the power that supports your intentions, makes you move things in a good direction, and causes yourself or someone else to receive your care. And everything continues going on the right path when your will unites with *Kuyay*, the tender affection with which the words come out of your mouth and you do your tasks.

"Respect people in countries that have the will to continue to develop and improve technology, but remember that the fact that they can build houses on other planets has no importance right now. For a long time, humanity has expanded outward on the basis of the power of technology to conquer the natural world while causing it much damage. But now the time has come for a change in direction. It is your task to expand inwardly, toward the black light that lives inside the seeds that the Universe is depositing in your interior. Caring for the integrity of your 'sacred pot'—your body, the container of your light—you will become like a greenhouse full of seedlings, and sooner or later you will see wisdom sprout from your own interior. A wisdom that will permit you to come into balance again with the natural world. As a survivor of a damaged time, it may be that, in the beginning, this new time wants you to recalibrate the connection of your mind (thoughts) with your body (nature) so that you may return to enjoying bodily awareness of the natural rhythms and so you can again flow naturally. This means that you will pass through a time of purification that will be difficult but will not last forever. Your body will ache, your mind will lose structure, and how to be yourself will become unclear. But just wait and endure, holding on to something sacred, until you start experiencing a better version of yourself."

These are instructions that I received from the spirit world, which I accepted without resisting. I looked around and found that so many of us were going through the same transformations, with or without being aware of it. And I felt that, unless these instructions were followed by a large part of the world's population, they could be useless in terms of healing the world. I wonder if it will be possible, on a large scale, for human beings to improve the way we use our minds. Because I have noticed that the people of the modern world, more intellectual than intuitive, tend to relate to the ideas they have about things and no longer know how to be in direct relationship with things themselves. The world exists in their heads rather than in what is right in front of them. Is it possible that this can change? One day a brother from another country who was becoming a good friend came to see me. He was very affected by these same questions, tired of feeling himself separated from the beauty of the world. He had a great spiritual hunger and was searching for something different. I remember him asking me, "What can we do to change, those of us who have lost the memory of the original design for good living?" And aware that I didn't have an answer for such a big question, I managed to not go to my head and look for one. I just responded spontaneously, "My brother, stop dedicating yourselves with so much enthusiasm to digging the holes you are going to fall into. Stop for a moment, brother, stop so much doing. Look, brother, let's share some food, and let's taste the earth." I passed him some *Kuka* leaves and said to him: "*Hallpaykusunchis wayq'echay*" (Let us be the land—with tender affection—for our benefit, my little brother). And after a long silence, I smiled and said to him, "*Saksachikuy wawq'ey,*" which means "Make yourself satiated with tender affection for your benefit, my brother."

ACKNOWLEDGMENTS

❖

Bacilio Zea Sánchez, my brother of heart, I thank you for your important participation in the creation of this work. Without our profound conversations and your sharing of what you have learned about our ancient culture, this book would be missing very precious content. Thank you for accompanying me so willingly in this harvest of ancestral wisdom. May your work, your students, and our people benefit from this sacred transmission that you helped me make.

Manari Ushigua, my jungle brother, thanks to you too, for the conversations that we had in our dreams, in the spirit world, on the phone, and in person. Your wisdom, and your father's wisdom, are very present in this work, and I feel very honored, brother.

Maisa Arias, Ricardo Chumpitazi, and Claudia Oré, I thank you for reading my first draft in Spanish. Your observations were very helpful. Your honest comments showed me the way to revise, again and again.

Peter Bokor, thanks so much for reading my manuscript and translating it to English—twice! I can imagine the first time around that my draft must have given you a hard time. And still you saw the potential of this work and were willing to translate it a second time when it was ripe. Your feedback and encouragement were very helpful to me, Peter. You saw how this book could be of service to people of our Andean countries and to people from different cultures who want our Mother Earth to be well cared for. Your unconditional support was very meaningful to me.

Michelle Puckett, what an honor it is for me, after so many years of developing yourself as the excellent editor that you are, that you accepted the challenge (for the first time) to edit a whole book. Thank you so much for respecting my voice and my culture the way you did.

Ginny Jordan, thank you, my dear friend, for always supporting my life's mission, my work. For so many years we have walked in the same direction with the same joys and pains, loving the Earth, never giving up.

Marilyn and Agatha—my dear loves, my wife and daughter—thank you for living with me at home, smiling instead of losing your patience all those times when I looked like my mind was somewhere else. But it was here, in the world that these words attempt to keep alive, our wonderful, ancient, and sacred world. I am very grateful for the warm world I live in with you.

GLOSSARY OF
QUECHUA WORDS

❖

Altomisayoq: A highly developed and gifted holy person and healer of the Andes; the one who has the highest altar.

Apu: Something or someone with a great and powerful spirit; protector, and sacred benefactor of Andean communities.

Apukuna: Plural of Apu.

Ayar Auqa: One of the four Ayar brothers. "*Auqa*" means "warrior."

Ayar Kachi: One of the four Ayar brothers. "*Kachi*" means "salt."

Ayar Manqo: One of the four Ayar brothers. "*Manqo*" means "pot."

Ayar Uchu: One of the four Ayar brothers. "*Uchu*" means "chili pepper."

Ayllu: A group of people that live together, organized as a community.

Ayni: Reciprocity.

Chaki Watana: Anklet.

Ch'ipana: Bracelet.

Ch'ullo: A soft traditional hat of the Andes.

Chumpi: Waistband.

Hallpa: Land.

Hallpaykusunchis: Let's be the land with tenderness for our benefit.

Hamautakuna: Teachers.

Hanaq Pacha: The world of the above.

Hanpichikuy: Make yourself healed with tenderness for your benefit.

Hawaq Pacha: Outer space.

Hawkay: Total fulfillment; plenitude.

Illa: A form of dim light; a ray of light.

Inka: A crystalized man. The main ruler, also called Sapan Inka.

Inti: Sun.

Intiwatana: Something used to tie the Sun.

Kallpa: Strength.

Kay: To be; here.

Kay Pacha: The middle world (this world) where we live.

Khuya: A sacred stone.

Kon: A great sacred power.

Kukamama: Coca leaf.

Kuyay: Tender affection.

Leq'echu: A type of seagull that lives near Andean lakes.

LLawtu: Headband.

Lloq'empa: Word of Aimara origin that means "tilting to the left."

Mama Ipakura: One of the Ayar sisters. "*Ipakura*" means "the older aunt."

Mama Oqllo: One of the Ayar sisters. "*Oqllo*" comes from "*Oqlloy*," which means "to incubate."

Mama Rewe: One of the Ayar sisters. "*Rewe*" means "ovum."

Mama Wak'o: One of the Ayar sisters. "*Wak'o*" is a word that refers to anyone or anything that contains something sacred.

Manqa: Pot.

Manqo: Pot.

Moraya: A type of dried potato.

Munay: Will of the heart; to want.

Muray: To make something change.

Ñaupa: The past; the space in front of us.

Pacha: Time; space; time-space.

Pachakamaq: The ordering principle of time-space.

Pachakuti: A turn in time-space; a return in time-space.

Pachamama: Mother Time-Space.

Pampamisayoq: The healer and spiritual leader who carries the altar of the land.

Paq'o: Healer; a ceremonial leader who prepares offerings.

Qatachillay: Constellation known in the Andes as "The Eyes of the Llama."

Q'espisqa Kay: Crystalized, liberated.

Qolla: Crystalized woman.

Quena: Andean flute.

Runa: Human being; an authentic human being.

Runasimi: The tongue of the human being.

Saksachikuy: Make yourself satiated with tenderness for your benefit.

Salqa: Wild.

Samay: Rest; to breathe; breath; to blow with purpose.

Seq'e: Line; invisible lines.

Titiqaqa Lake: On the border between Peru and Bolivia.

Uchukuta: Sauce made with chili peppers.

Ukhu Pacha: Underworld.

Unucha: From "*Unu*," which means "water." The suffix "*cha*" works as a diminutive that adds tenderness and affection to the word.

Wak'a: Someone, something, or a space that contains a powerful sacred energy.

Wakcha: Poor person, understood in Andean culture as someone who doesn't have a community.

Walthay: To wrap; to bring the energy back to the center.

Wanka: Standing rock.

Waq'a: Mentally insane.

Watana: Something that serves to tie.

Wawq'echay: My little brother. The diminutive expresses affection.

Wawq'ey: My brother.

Willka: Sacred.

Willaq: The one who tells.

Yachaywasi: House of wisdom.

Yakana: One of the names of the constellation of "The Eyes of the Llama."

Yanantin: Two beings that create a complement thanks to their differences.

Yuyaq: The one who remembers; a thinker, or one who understands.

Yuyay: To remember; to think, or to understand.

Zampoña: A pan flute originating in the area of the Altiplano, around Lake Titiqaqa.

BIBLIOGRAPHY

❖

De Avila, Francisco, *Gods and Men of Huarochirí*, trans. Jose Maria Arguedas.

Figueroa, Juan Carlos Machicado, *When the Stones Speak* (Cusco: Inka 2000, 2002).

Hurtado, Federico Garcia, and Pilar Roca Palacio, *Pachakuteq* (2020).

Luiselli, Alessandra, *Instruccin Del Inca Don Diego de Castro Titu Cusi Yupanqui* (2001).

Ordazábal, Mario Osorio, *The Legacy of the Ancestral Andean Society* (2011).

Pease, Franklin, *Curacas, Reciprocity and Wealth* (Lima: Pontificia Universidad Católica del Perú, 1992).

Pease, Franklin, *The Incas* (Lima: Pontificia Universidad Católica del Perú, 2015).

Soliz, Ruth Shady, *The Caral-Supe Civilization, Five Thousand Years of Cultural Identity in Peru* (Lima: Proyecto Especial Arqueológico Caral-Supe/I.N.C, 2005).

Villena, Carlos Milla, *Ayni* (Lima: Amaru Wayra, 2004).

About the Author

❖

I was born in Arequipa, at the foot of the Misti volcano. My parents entered my name into the public registers as Pablo Hernán Quiñones Lavarello, and my family and friends always called me Hernán. I received the name Arkan Lushwala as an adult in one of the times I was consecrated to be a spiritual servant.

As a young child, I lived with my family in Chiclayo, and then we went to live in the port of Callao. My parents were chalacos. My father was a mestizo, descended from Indigenous people from northern Peru on his mother's side and from Indigenous people from southern Peru on his father's side, who also had African and Spanish blood. My mother also had blood from the Indigenous of northern Peru, but she did not look like them in appearance. My mom and her brothers had a great-grandfather who was Italian, and so they were of white complexion and identified themselves as white people. With this mixture of races inside me, as has been the case for many people from my country, it was difficult for me to decide on my ethnic identity. If I told an inhabitant from an Andean community that I was descended from the Indigenous, they told me I was white. If I told a white person that I had an Italian great-grandfather, they would not believe me. Once, I went to Italy and people there noticed immediately my Andean roots, and when I told them I had an Italian great-grandfather, they believed it less than if I had told them I could fly. In my case, as in the case of many others—Peruvians, Ecuadorians, Colombians, Mexicans, Chileans, and in general people from all the countries now called Latin America—my ethnic identity had to be my choice. And I am grateful to have been able to realize that choosing to be a descendant of Indigenous people implies an enormous commitment. A lot depends on the way one chooses to live, on the language one uses to see the world through, and on how one relates to Mother Earth. I had ancestral treasure stored in my genetic memory that woke up at a very young age, but at the same time I had to expose myself constantly to the example and guidance of people who had grown up, since birth, in a purely Indigenous environment. As a child I enjoyed traveling to villages in my country where people received me with affection and infected me with their way of being. I also enjoyed spending time in the dark kitchen whose thatched walls were blackened from soot in the home of my paternal grandmother, and it was enchanting to watch her and her sister cook, with their long braids tied behind their backs. But strangely, it was my destiny to go deeply into the sacred aspect of my Indigenous being with the help of natives from North American tribes as well.

My first encounter with Indigenous brothers and sisters from the north of our continent occurred when I was nineteen. One day, I was working in Lima when I suddenly received a tempting call from a good friend who was going to Cusco to a meeting of Indigenous people from the whole continent. Immediately, I quit work, and on the following day I was flying with my friend on a cargo plane from the Peruvian Air Force, knowing I had enough money to go but not to return. Two days later I found myself at the side of Indigenous people from many different nations, in front of a stone altar in Ollantaytambo, watching a Navajo elder pray to the sacred water that was flowing from this Inkan altar after having blessed the four directions of the world, the sky, and the Earth, with a feather that came from an eagle that had been flying in the skies of Arizona. For some reason that I could not understand at that moment, I felt profoundly moved, and I knew that my life was going to change, as if I were an amnesiac beginning to remember or like a man who had gotten lost and then suddenly found the road home. But I did not go home immediately. The road was long. In spite of knowing that my grandmother had come to Lima from the highlands of Trujillo, where our ancestors the descendants of the ancient Muchik nation lived, I did not have the conviction that I was Indigenous. It was not until years later when someone invited me to walk as a true Indigenous person. This was a good man named Aurelio Diaz Tekpankalli, a Purepekcha native from Mexico. After having met in a peyote ceremony that took place in Lima, Aurelio invited me to come to a place in Mexico where he "put people on the mountain," a place where he helped people do a Lakota Vision Quest ritual that he had done with the Crow Dog family in South Dakota years before. It was clear that I wanted to say yes, that this was the best invitation I had ever received in my life, but at first it occurred to me to tell him that I was mestizo, that I had both Indigenous blood as well as blood of European origin. Aurelio looked me in the eye, with both affection and firmness, and asked me not to insult myself by calling myself mestizo. He told me that the grandchildren of the Indigenous could be Indigenous if they accepted themselves as such. And fortunately, being a young enthusiast, and daring as I was at that age, I accepted.

After having visited Mexico for five consecutive years to do Vision Quest ceremonies under the guidance of Tekpankalli, I finally moved to New Mexico in the United States, where I settled into a relationship of profound friendship with an elder Apache named Servando Trujillo, who also had a close relationship with spiritual leaders of the Lakota tribe. With my uncle Servando, I traveled from New Mexico to South Dakota many times to visit the Lakota who were friends of his. I had the honor of meeting many wise people. I learned a lot about the art of conducting sacred ceremonies from Uncle Servando, without him teaching me but by working and observing while he offered Lakota rituals on New Mexican land. My uncle Servando left this world in the same year that Basil Brave Heart came into my life, a medicine man from the Oglala Lakota tribe in Pine Ridge, South Dakota. Shortly after we met, he told me that I was his son, and he adopted me in a traditional ceremony. With my father Basil, I became a Sun Dancer, enjoyed the powerful *Yuwipi* ceremonies, in which the veil between our world and the spirit world completely disappears, and did what I could to learn from his good example—to be the best a man can be as he becomes someone who offers medicine and ceremonies to people and at the same time needs to fulfill his responsibilities for his family and community. During the years I worked in New Mexico as a ceremonial leader in the Lakota tradition with the permission of Basil Brave Heart, I was able to continue my relationship with my place of origin, traveling a lot, always coming and going. It was the honor of my life to learn, in Cusco, from my dear *tayta*, a Pampamisayoq from the Q'ero nation named Martin Paucar Ccapac. Throughout many years he showed my brothers, Miguel Angel Pimentel and Bacilio Zea Sánchez, and me a beautiful way of preparing offerings to *Pachamama* and the *Apus*.

Last and most importantly, I give my thanks to the community of Ccotataki, whose people, now my family, gave me the immense gift of making me a member of their community up high in the mountains of the Sacred Valley of Cusco.

Arkan Lushwala
Taray, Cusco, December 2022